Teacher's Ma
Resource Book

manual
2 ...7

101 American English Idioms

Harry Collis

Illustrations by Mario Risso

National Textbook Company
a division of NTC/CONTEMPORARY PUBLISHING GROUP
Lincolnwood, Illinois USA

ISBN: 0-8442-5457-6

Published by National Textbook Company,
a division of NTC/Contemporary Publishing Group, Inc.
4255 West Touhy Avenue,
Lincolnwood (Chicago), Illinois 60712-1975 U.S.A.
© 1988 by NTC/Contemporary Publishing Group, Inc.

00 01 02 03 04 ML 12 11 10 9 8 7

Contents

Acknowledgments

I should like to express my profound gratitude to my wife, Katherine, for her ever-present support and creative input.

My appreciation also goes to my children, Marika, Denise, and Gregory, for their inspired contributions to the improvisational scenarios for the manual, and to Jackie Appell for her help with the word games.

I am particularly grateful to Michael Ross, my editor, whose incisive suggestions formed the basis for the writing of this work.

Introduction

The *101 American English Idioms Learning Cards* are designed to promote understanding and spontaneous, appropriate usage of 101 of the most commonly used American English idioms. Each card contains an illustration that depicts the literal meaning of the idiom in a lively, humorous style. On the back of each card is a dialogue or short passage that uses the idiom—plus its "translation"—in a natural context. These dialogues and passages will help to teach the actual meanings of the idioms, while the illustrations will increase students' comprehension and retention of the expressions by highlighting the contrast between their literal and actual meanings. In addition, the illustrations will serve as a springboard for vocabulary development and spontaneous conversation.

The cards are numbered and grouped into nine sections based on the meanings of the idioms. However, they may be used in any order, since the contextualizing passages are not progressive in difficulty.

This Teacher's Manual and Resource Book contains discussion questions, exercises, and activities for use in teaching the idioms, as well as a complete alphabetical listing of all the idioms included on the cards. Many of the exercises are presented in the form of blackline masters, which can be removed from the manual and photocopied for classroom use.

Getting the Ball Rolling

The material in this manual is divided into nine sections that correspond to the arrangement of the cards in the box. For each idiom, two sets of questions are provided to aid in eliciting and guiding conversation about the elements of the illustration, and to promote an instinctive feeling for the idiom by using related imagery. The wording of the questions is natural and often idiomatic in order to expand further the students' vocabulary and to give them a feeling for the colloquial phrasing of questions. The first set of questions, titled *What's Going On?,* focuses directly on the elements of the idiom as it is depicted in the illustration. The second set of questions—*The Ball's in Your Court*—focuses on expansion of vocabulary and ideas that go beyond the idiom itself, encouraging students to talk "around" the situation presented in the illustration.

Next, the idiom is reinforced in the form of a brief contextualizing passage and a follow-up question *(It's Up to You)*. Students may be asked to answer the question individually (orally or in writing) or to discuss their answers in small groups or with the entire class.

Finally, a *Toot Your Own Horn* or *Play It by Ear* section is provided for each idiom. These sections contain a longer description of a situation, which should be read aloud or copied and distributed to the students. The students must then prepare a response to or presentation of the situation, generally in the form of a skit or a written or oral dialogue or monologue. The activities in these sections are well-suited for group and pair work.

With imagination on the part of the students and teacher, there is ample room for expansion of vocabulary and imagery within the framework of the activities provided for each idiom. Some questions might even be assigned as homework, since they could well require the use of a dictionary or other method of research. It is not necessary to have all students answer all the questions in the *What's Going On?* and *The Ball's in Your Court* sections. Depending on the students' abilities or levels of achievement, you can select questions that are within the realm of their control or even slightly more challenging.

All's Well That Ends Well

At the end of each section, a set of review activities *(All's Well That Ends Well)* is presented on blackline masters. These activities include multiple-choice, fill-in-the-blank, and matching exercises, as well as word-game activities such as crossword puzzles and word searches. The pages in this section are designed to be removed from the manual, photocopied, and distributed to the students. The activities may be completed in class, with students working individually or in small groups, or assigned for homework. Some teachers may even wish to use them for testing purposes. Answer keys for all the activities are provided at the end of the section.

Give It Your Best Shot

Below are some suggestions for presenting the idioms with the help of the learning cards. These suggestions are intended only as general guidelines, since working with the cards is certain to inspire many other workable ideas.

1. While holding up a card, ask the students to comment on what they see. They may wish to talk about the individual elements of the picture or about the situation itself. This can be an entirely free discussion, providing ample opportunity for expansion of vocabulary and grammar.

2. Try to lead the students to the meaning of the idiom by highlighting its relationship to the situation portrayed in the illustration.

3. At this point, you might try reading aloud the dialogue or passage printed on the back of the learning card, explaining vocabulary and grammar as necessary to insure comprehension. After hearing the dialogue, the students could experiment with paraphrasing the situation presented in the dialogue.

4. Conclude this part of the discussion by asking the students some or all of the questions from the *What's Going On?* and *The Ball's in Your Court* sections of the Teacher's Manual.

5. Present the material from the *It's Up to You* section and have the students answer the question orally or in writing.

6. Present the situation described in the *Toot Your Own Horn* or *Play It by Ear* section to the students. Working in pairs, groups, or individually, the students will prepare skits or dialogues based on the situation.

After you've covered all the idioms in a particular section:

7. Select exercises and activities from the *All's Well That Ends Well* section to duplicate and distribute to the students.

8. Play a review game, "Let's Play Round Robin," with the flash cards. The purpose of the game is to have all the students in the class contribute to the development of a skit or story based on the idioms in one section. Divide the class into pairs or teams in such a way that you have an equal number of idioms per team. Put all the learning cards from the section in a bag or box with tall sides. Have one student from the first team close his or her eyes, draw a card from the bag, and show it to the class. He and the other members of his team must then begin to improvise a dialogue or skit in which the idiom could be used, or make up a story based on the idiom.

On a signal from you, someone from that team must point to the members of another team, indicating that they must immediately take over the development of the dialogue, skit, or story. Again, on a signal from you, the members of the second team must choose a third team to take up the conversation and develop it as the members' imaginations and vocabulary permit. The "round robin" rotation should continue until each team has contributed its ideas. Then a student from the second team starts the process again by drawing a new card from the bag. The game continues until a story has been developed for each idiom in the bag.

A panel of judges (one student from each team) should be selected to "judge" the teams for spontaneity, originality, and imagination—with you providing your opinions on the usage of language and structures. The winning team should receive an appropriate "prize" such as a night without homework or a class period in which to do free reading. This game should both challenge the students and provide them with a sense of accomplishment.

In addition to the Learning Cards and this Teacher's Manual, National Textbook Company publishes a book titled *101 American English Idioms*. This book contains the same 101 idioms found on the learning cards; in fact, the card numbers correspond to the page numbers on which the idioms appear in the book. Each idiom appears on a separate page in the book, complete with the illustration and dialogue or passage shown on the learning card. Thus, the book may be used in conjunction with or as an alternative to the learning cards. The questions, activities, and exercises provided in this Teacher's Manual are appropriate for use with either the cards or the book.

In addition to the steps for teaching the idioms outlined above, you might wish to incorporate the following activities if the students in your class have copies of the *101 American English Idioms* book:

1. Read aloud each line of the dialogue or passage, having the students repeat after you in groups, pairs, or individually.

2. Have the students read the dialogue or passage and study the picture for a particular idiom, then ask them to think of a situation that is similar to the one described in the book.

3. Ask the students if they can think of "parallel" idioms in their native languages. If they can, have them translate the expressions literally into English and discuss the differences between the various versions of an idiom. This would make a good vocabulary and culture activity.

4. Have the students memorize part or all of a dialogue or passage for homework, or have them write a new dialogue or passage based on the idiom.

Clearly, the focus of the *101 American English Idioms* Learning Cards, Teacher's Manual, and book is the development of spontaneous oral expression. It is the hope of the author that the activities contained herein will lead students to develop the instinct that is so necessary for natural, idiomatic discourse in American English.

Alphabetical Listing of Idioms

Section One

It's a Zoo Out There

1. Smell a Rat

What's Going On?   Ask the class the following questions:

What is the man doing? Why? What is he holding? What is the man wearing? Where is he? Is he happy with what he's doing? Do you see anything wrong?

The Ball's in Your Court   Ask the class the following questions:

What is the man's occupation? What kitchen utensils is he using? Name some other kitchen utensils. How are they used in preparing different kinds of foods? Under what circumstances might you smell a rat? How would you feel? The rat is a rodent. Describe a rodent. Do you know of any other common rodents?

It's Up to You   Present this situation to the students for discussion:

If you were the manager of a store and found that money was missing from the cash register at the end of every day, what would you say about the situation?

Toot Your Own Horn   Have the students compose (orally or in writing) a skit or dialogue based on the following situation:

This week the class is to be tested on English grammar. The teacher gives a rather difficult examination, and after correcting it she discovers that every student got a perfect paper.

2. Go to the Dogs

What's Going On?   Ask the class the following questions:

Where is the dog? What is he doing? What has "gone to the dogs"? In what way? Is the dog anxious to have his house repaired? Comment on the condition of the doghouse.

The Ball's in Your Court   Ask the class the following questions:

What other things can become run-down? (People can become run-down, too.) Can you think of ways in which a person can become run-down? What words would you use to describe people or things that "go to the dogs"? Name some other household pets.

It's Up to You   Present this situation to the students for discussion:

Joe used to be a very neat, well-groomed person. However, he has not been keeping up his appearance and now looks quite shabby. What would you say about him if you saw him in his present condition?

Play It by Ear   Have the students compose (orally or in writing) a speech or monologue based on the following situation:

Pretend that you are a tourist guide talking about your city or town. Mention not only the positive aspects of the city or town (museums, parks, etc.), but the negative aspects as well.

3. Fishy

What's Going On?   Ask the class the following questions:

What is the fish wearing? What does this make you think about the fish? What is the fish doing? Does the grandfather clock belong to the fish? Idiomatically speaking, what comparison can be drawn between the fish and the rat in *smell a rat*? Explain. Is a fish out of water a common occurrence? What does the facial expression of the fish suggest to you? If you saw a man wearing a mask, what would you think? In your opinion, would the man necessarily be doing something wrong?

The Ball's in Your Court　Ask the class the following questions:

Do you know the names of other fish? Name some other types of sea animals. Can you describe them? Do fish walk? What do they do? What do other sea animals do? Where? In what ways are fish useful to people? How would you react if you saw a suspicious character? Have you ever had reason to be suspicious of someone? If so, describe the situation.

It's Up to You　Present this situation to the students for discussion:

What would you say if you were in a parking lot and saw a man going around trying to open the locked doors of the cars on the lot?

Play It by Ear　Have the students compose (orally or in writing) a skit or dialogue based on the following situation:

You are working as a helper in a big hospital. Lately you have noticed that many patients have been developing strange symptoms after taking a certain brand of aspirin. To whom would you go with this information, and how would you explain it?

4. Take the Bull by the Horns

What's Going On?　Ask the class the following questions: What is the woman holding on to? How is she dressed? What is she doing? Have you ever seen a bull? Are bulls usually very friendly? Would it be easy or hard to grab ahold of a bull's horns?

The Ball's in Your Court　Ask the class the following questions:

Why do bulls have horns? Name some other animals that have horns. Where do bulls usually live? Would a bull make a good pet? Why or why not? Can you think of a sport that involves bulls? Have you ever seen a bullfight? If so, describe it.

It's Up to You　Present this situation to the students for discussion:

Bill is a hard worker who does his job well. He is frustrated because he has never been given a promotion, even though he has worked for the same company for twelve years. Bill's boss has a reputation for being difficult to talk to. What would you advise Bill to do?

Toot Your Own Horn　Have the students compose (orally or in writing) a skit or dialogue based on the following situation:

Your apartment has gotten very crowded and everyone in the family is complaining about the lack of space. One day you get tired of all the complaints and go to look for a bigger place to live. A few days later you meet a friend at the supermarket and tell her that you and your family are moving to a house on the other side of town. How would you explain your decision to move?

5. Horse of a Different Color

What's Going On?   Ask the class the following questions:

What is the man doing to the horse? Is this a common thing to do? What does the man have in his hand? Will this horse be like other horses? In what ways will it be the same? In what ways will it be different? What might the horse think about what the man is doing?

The Ball's in Your Court   Ask the class the following questions:

What are horses used for? Is it an advantge or a disadvantage to be different in some way? What are some of the pros and cons of being different? What color do you think the man is painting the horse? Name some other colors. What do horses eat? Do you know where horses live, or where they can be kept? Name some other animals and tell how they are different from each other.

It's Up to You   Present this situation to the students for discussion:

In a store, you see something that you want to have but cannot afford to buy. How would you describe the relationship between your desire to possess it and your inability to actually own it?

Toot Your Own Horn   Have the students compose (orally or in writing) a dialogue based on the following situation:

Imagine that you have a friend who has always wanted to be a pilot. He has undergone strenuous training and has finally received his diploma and license as a commercial airline pilot. He comes to you and complains that, although he is qualified, he cannot find a job. What would you tell him?

6. Let the Cat Out of the Bag

What's Going On?   Ask the class the following questions:

How does the man feel about what he has done? Is he sorry? What type of cat is in the bag? How does the cat feel? Do you think that the man made a mistake by freeing the cat? How did he free the cat? What do you think the cat will do? Do you think the man would have freed the cat if he had known what kind of cat it was? Explain.

The Ball's in Your Court   Ask the class the following questions:

Is it hard or easy to keep a secret? Why? Have you ever revealed something you weren't supposed to? What happened? Is this the type of cat you would have as a household pet? Explain. Can you name other kinds of cats? Where are they usually found? Do you prefer a cat to a dog? Why?

It's Up to You   Present this situation to the students for discussion:

What would you say to someone who told you about the time and place of a surprise party that was being planned for you?

Play It by Ear   Have the students compose (orally or in writing) a skit or dialogue based on the following situation:

Your friend Tom has not see his married sister for a long time. She has been living far away in another part of the country. She plans to come for a visit and drop in on Tom unannounced, since she wants to surprise him with the news that she is expecting a baby. Unfortunately, the married sister reveals this information to her mother without telling her to keep the information confidential. The mother then inadvertently reveals the news about the pregnancy to Tom.

7. For the Birds

What's Going On? Ask the class the following questions:

What is the big bird doing? Is the man interested in what is going on? What do his eyes tell you? Compare the attitude of the man with that of the two other birds. Who seems more interested in the reading? What kind of reading is it?

The Ball's in Your Court Ask the class the following questions:

How do you react to something uninteresting? Do you walk away from it? Are you polite when someone is telling you something that you find boring? What do you do when you are bored? What are some of the things that interest or bore you? A wren is a bird. Describe a bird. What is the difference between a bird and an animal that does not fly? What advantage does the bird have by being able to fly? Is an animal that cannot fly at a disadvantage? Name some other types of birds. Does poetry interest you? Why or why not? What types of literature interest you the most? What types of cultural activities interest you? What types of cultural activities bore you?

It's Up to You Present this situation to the students for discussion:

As a present for your birthday, someone has just given you a book that you thoroughly dislike. How would you express your opinion of the book? Would you say this to the giver, or to someone else?

Toot Your Own Horn Have the students compose (orally or in writing) a skit or dialogue based on the following situation:

Your parents want to introduce you to the delights of classical music by taking you to a symphony concert. You are fifteen years old and at this point in your life the only kind of music you like is rock and roll. You discuss the situation with some of your friends and ask them to help you find a way to get out of going with your folks without hurting their feelings.

8. Straight From the Horse's Mouth

What's Going On? Ask the class the following questions:

What type of horse do you see in the illustration? Describe it. What information is the horse revealing? What is the man doing? Why is the man paying such close attention to the horse? Would this particular horse be in a position to reveal something that the man would believe? Explain. Who is the man taking down the information? Why do you suppose he wants to know what the horse is telling him? Is the horse a good source for this type of information? Why or why not?

The Ball's in Your Court Ask the class the following questions:

Can horses talk? Is *talk* the right word to use for the sounds that a horse makes? What sound does a horse make? Describe the sounds that dogs, cats, cows, birds, and other animals make. Do you know why people are interested in going to horse races? What do we call people who ride horses? What do we call people who ride horses in races? When you receive information about the English language from your teacher, do you believe her? Why or why not? Can you name some other sources of information? Are they reliable? Explain. Who is in a position to provide dependable information?

It's Up to You   Present this situation to the students for discussion:

Your most trusted friend comes to you with an almost unbelievable piece of news. Would you believe what you were told? How would you express the fact that you accepted the information as true?

Play It by Ear   Have the students compose (orally or in writing) a skit or dialogue based on the following situation:

You have been investing in the stock market for a number of years. Although you have not lost any money, you have never "made a killing." Your stockbroker, who has been your trusted friend and who has always given you sound advice on your investments, comes to you with the name of a company and recommends that you invest a good deal of money in this company. Describe the situation to a friend and tell him what you would or would not do and why.

9. Horse Around

What's Going On?   Ask the class the following questions:

What is unusual about this horse? What is he doing to the woman? How is she reacting? Would you say that the man/horse is being playful? Do you think he intends to hurt the woman? What are his intentions? Is the woman interested in playing a game with him? What does her facial expression tell you? What is the woman wearing around her head? How is she dressed? In what type of place are they? Is the man an ordinary man? Explain. What do you think he was doing before he saw the woman? What does the fact that he abandoned his previous activity tell you?

The Ball's in Your Court   Ask the class the following questions:

What do you do for exercise? Do both men and women use bar bells? For what purpose? Do you ever feel playful? On what occasions? Have you ever teased anybody? Why? How did they react? Do you always have a reason for behaving the way you do?

It's Up to You   Present this situation to the students for discussion:

If you knew a student who was not being serious about his studies and preferred to engage in unproductive activities, what would you tell this person?

Toot Your Own Horn   Have the students write or improvise orally a skit based on the following situation:

John and Bill have always been good, serious students. Their teachers have always admired their positive attitude concerning their studies. All of a sudden, for no apparent reason, they begin missing classes and their grades start to go down. Many of their friends see them in the local billiard hall or wandering aimlessly in the streets. How would you explain their behavior?

10. Cat Got Your Tongue?

What's Going On?   Ask the class the following questions:

Why is the man distressed? How did the cat manage to get ahold of the man's tongue? Why do you suppose the cat is holding his tongue? How would you say the cat is feeling? How can you tell? Does the man still have his power of speech? In what position has the cat placed the man?

The Ball's in Your Court   Ask the class the following questions:

Under what circumstances might a person be unable to utter a word? Under what circumstances might a person be talkative? What do we call a person who cannot talk? What do we call a person who cannot hear? Have you ever been rendered speechless? How did it happen? Do cats usually make people lose their ability to speak? What is the normal relationship between a cat and a person? How do cats and people interact? How would you feel if someone tried to grab your tongue?

It's Up to You   Present this situation to the students for discussion:

Imagine that a friend of yours stopped in the middle of a sentence while telling you about his vacation. You prompted him to continue, but he couldn't. What would you ask him as you tried to get him to continue?

Play It by Ear   Have the students compose (orally or in writing) a skit based on the following situation:

You are attending a formal dinner and the featured speaker is a well-known politician. However, she seems to be having trouble expressing herself when members of the audience express their dissatisfaction with some of her legislation. She is constantly being put on the spot, and begins to stutter and stammer. At times she can't even come up with a satisfactory response and has to stop to collect her thoughts.

All's Well That Ends Well

I. Select the best idiom to complete each sentence. In some cases, more than one answer is possible.

1. The owners of that house are on vacation, and there's a light on in the living room. Very frankly,

   _____.
   a. that's for the birds
   b. I smell a rat
   c. someone must have let the cat out of the bag

2. Wanting to travel is one thing, but being able to do so is_____

   _____.
   a. fishy
   b. straight from the horse's mouth
   c. a horse of a different color

3. How come you don't want to tell us what happened with Bea last night? What's the matter?

   _____
   a. Cat got your tongue?
   b. Did someone let the cat out of the bag?
   c. Was your date for the birds?

4. Everybody came home early from the art exhibition last night. That's too bad. I guess_____

   _____.
   a. it was a horse of a different color
   b. it must have been for the birds
   c. they took the bull by the horns

5. You'll never get anyplace if you keep_____.
   a. taking the bull by the horns
   b. horsing around
   c. going to the dogs

6. At one time the children's playground was really nice, but now hardly anyone goes there because

   _____.
   a. everyone was horsing around
   b. it has gone to the dogs
   c. it's for the birds

7. Did you hear that Frank joined the Air Force? I'm glad he finally _____

   and told his parents he didn't want to go to college.
   a. went to the dogs
   b. got it straight from the horse's mouth
   c. took the bull by the horns

8. "Who says they had an argument? They *never* argue." "Well, I happen to know because_____

_____."

   a. I was horsing around

   b. someone let the cat out of the bag

   c. I got it straight from the horse's mouth

9. "How did you find out they were planning to elope?" "Actually, no one was supposed to know,

but Margie, who's a good friend of theirs,_____."

   a. let the cat out of the bag

   b. smelled a rat

   c. got it straight from the horse's mouth

10. When she walked in her office and saw that the furniture had been moved while she was out, she

knew that_____.

   a. it had gone to the dogs

   b. something fishy had gone on

   c. someone had let the cat out of the bag

II. Match the situation in column A with the idiom in column B.

A	**B**
_____ 1. Why is she so quiet?	a. Yes. It had really gone to the dogs.
_____ 2. Who let him know that a banquet was being planned in his honor?	b. Two or three pages are missing. I smell a rat.
_____ 3. We didn't like his performance at all!	c. No. She finally took the bull by the horns and told him she wanted to date someone else.
_____ 4. The Smiths were certain that something strange and suspicious was going on.	d. Who knows? I guess the cat's got her tongue.
_____ 5. They couldn't believe that the neighborhood looked so miserable.	e. I'm not sure. Marcia probably let the cat out of the bag.
_____ 6. Roller-skating is easy, but skiing is something else again.	f. It really was for the birds!
_____ 7. Why are you shuffling through those papers? Is something wrong?	g. So stop horsing around and get serious!
_____ 8. I haven't seen Tom and Sarah together lately, have you?	h. I agree. You might say that it's a horse of a different color.
_____ 9. How are you so sure that Jerry got the promotion?	i. Yeah! It sure looked fishy to me, too.
_____ 10. You'll get into trouble if you keep playing around that way.	j. To tell you the truth, I got it straight from the horse's mouth.

III. Find and circle the following idioms. Be sure to look horizontally, vertically, and diagonally.

smell a rat   let the cat out of the bag
go to the dogs   for the birds
fishy   straight from (the) horse's mouth
take the bull by the horns   horse around
horse of a different color   cat got your tongue

s	l	e	t	t	h	e	c	a	t	o	u	t	o	f	t	h	e	b	a	g	z
t	a	r	q	a	b	h	y	n	t	s	i	r	k	j	m	n	t	c	h	a	r
r	z	t	s	k	e	y	u	r	n	d	f	l	h	g	c	a	o	v	p	w	a
a	n	c	x	e	w	h	r	a	n	b	a	c	d	l	h	i	h	r	g	t	l
i	f	l	r	t	k	s	m	e	l	l	a	r	a	t	b	c	n	y	d	h	h
g	r	h	i	h	u	i	x	c	j	d	o	l	b	a	t	x	r	n	e	s	o
h	o	r	s	e	o	f	a	d	i	f	f	e	r	e	n	t	c	o	l	o	r
t	b	l	n	b	h	g	l	p	q	n	r	f	e	b	c	p	a	d	n	l	s
f	s	h	o	u	l	a	x	p	t	b	q	y	m	j	p	n	t	r	s	p	e
r	h	l	i	l	w	t	v	b	y	d	u	a	h	n	g	r	g	l	t	b	a
o	l	d	e	l	w	r	s	h	e	n	l	t	y	q	x	r	o	n	b	a	r
m	o	h	j	b	e	f	x	t	l	e	b	t	s	h	b	c	t	v	u	a	o
h	y	n	d	y	g	l	i	q	h	r	h	n	d	b	d	o	y	u	k	d	u
o	b	d	o	t	o	h	r	t	l	n	b	c	r	d	x	t	o	v	u	w	n
r	k	h	r	h	t	l	n	e	h	l	d	y	i	c	t	b	u	n	d	k	d
s	r	t	f	e	o	o	x	y	w	b	d	v	b	r	l	n	r	c	b	i	e
e	h	c	r	h	t	d	l	i	j	b	l	c	e	n	m	a	t	d	e	o	e
s	k	p	r	o	h	l	d	v	t	u	w	c	h	x	z	r	o	p	p	d	i
m	a	c	e	r	e	d	g	p	t	y	s	c	t	g	h	x	n	z	p	r	o
o	b	k	i	n	d	h	r	n	o	s	v	u	r	l	n	o	g	c	d	e	f
u	a	j	l	s	o	l	o	n	d	t	o	m	o	f	o	r	u	t	l	x	a
t	k	r	n	j	g	o	c	d	p	h	m	g	f	r	t	a	e	b	t	s	y
h	c	t	y	m	s	t	b	o	l	k	d	c	q	u	k	c	h	l	m	n	a

Answer Key

I.   1. b   5. b   9. a
   2. c   6. b   10. b
   3. a or c   7. c
   4. b   8. c

II. 1. d   5. a   9. j
   2. e   6. h   10. g
   3. f   7. b
   4. i   8. c

III.

```
s  l  e  t  t  h  e  c  a  t  o  u  t  o  f  t  h  e  b  a  g  z
t  a  r  q  a  b  h  y  n  t  s  i  r  k  j  m  n  t  c  h  a  r
r  z  t  s  k  e  y  u  r  n  d  f  l  h  g  c  a  o  v  p  w  a
a  n  c  x  e  w  h  r  a  n  b  a  c  d  l  h  i  h  r  g  t  l
i  f  l  r  t  k  s  m  e  l  l  a  r  a  t  b  c  n  y  d  h  h
g  r  h  i  h  u  i  x  c  j  d  o  l  b  a  t  x  r  n  e  s  o
h  o  r  s  e  o  f  a  d  i  f  f  e  r  e  n  t  c  o  l  o  r
t  b  l  n  b  h  g  l  p  q  n  r  f  e  b  c  p  a  d  n  l  s
f  s  h  o  u  l  a  x  p  t  b  q  y  m  j  p  n  t  r  s  p  e
r  h  l  i  l  w  t  v  b  y  d  u  a  h  n  g  r  g  l  t  b  a
o  l  d  e  l  w  r  s  h  e  n  l  t  y  q  x  r  o  n  b  a  r
m  o  h  j  b  e  f  x  t  l  e  b  t  s  h  b  c  t  v  u  a  o
h  y  n  d  y  g  l  i  q  h  r  h  n  d  b  d  o  y  u  k  d  u
o  b  d  o  t  o  h  r  t  l  n  b  c  r  d  x  t  o  v  u  w  n
r  k  h  r  h  t  l  n  e  h  l  d  y  i  c  t  b  u  n  d  k  d
s  r  t  f  e  o  o  x  y  w  b  d  v  b  r  l  n  r  c  b  i  e
e  h  c  r  h  t  d  l  i  j  b  l  c  e  n  m  a  t  d  e  o  e
s  k  p  r  o  h  l  d  v  t  u  w  c  h  x  z  r  o  p  p  d  i
m  a  c  e  r  e  g  p  t  y  s  c  t  g  h  x  n  z  p  r  o
o  b  k  i  n  d  h  r  n  o  s  v  u  r  l  n  o  g  c  d  e  f
u  a  j  l  s  o  l  o  n  d  t  o  m  o  f  o  r  u  t  l  x  a
t  k  r  n  k  g  o  c  d  p  h  m  g  f  r  t  a  e  b  t  s  y
h  c  t  y  m  s  t  b  o  l  k  d  c  q  u  k  c  h  l  m  n  a
```

Section Two

The Body Has Many Uses

11. Get in Someone's Hair

What's Going On? Ask the class the following questions:

How would you say the woman is feeling? How can you tell? Describe the woman's hair. Where are the children? How are the children feeling? What are they doing?

The Ball's in Your Court Ask the class the following questions:

How do you feel when you have something in your hair? If you are annoyed, how do you react? When do you think the woman might *not* feel bothered by her children? When would she feel bothered? Have you ever felt annoyed by anyone? Can you describe the situation? Have you ever annoyed anyone? How did they react?

It's Up to You Present this situation to the students for discussion:

If you were trying to concentrate on your homework, and your little brother kept interrupting you, what would you tell him?

Toot Your Own Horn Have the students compose (orally or in writing) a skit based on the following situation:

Your father has been trying to do some repairs around the house. First your sister disturbs him from his work by asking him for help with some homework. Next you come to him and ask him to take you to your soccer game. Finally, your mother interrupts and asks him to go shopping with her. How do you think your father would express his frustration?

12. Shoot Off One's Mouth

What's Going On? Ask the class the following questions:

What do you think is coming out of the mouth of the man on the left? What is the man on the right doing? Why? How is he feeling? What do you think of the man on the left? Is he being quiet? Why do you suppose there is smoke?

The Ball's in Your Court Ask the class the following questions:

What verb is often used with the noun *pistol*? What does one hear when a pistol is fired? How do you react when you hear someone talking very loudly? What circumstances could have led to the scene shown in the picture? How do you think it will be resolved?

It's Up to You Present this situation to the students for discussion:

Although Eric is very bright, he's always talking loudly about his accomplishments. If Eric's attitude annoyed you, what would you ask him?

Play It by Ear Have the students compose (orally or in writing) a dialogue or skit based on the following situation:

John has quite a reputation for exaggeration. He's always talking about his achievements in sports and his many girlfriends. He acts as if he is an authority on any given subject. Describe some of the things he might say and how you would react to them.

13. Jump Down Someone's Throat

What's Going On?   Ask the class the following questions:

What is your first impression of this picture? How does the man who is jumping feel? Why do you think he would be trying to leap at the other man's throat? Is the other man happy with what's going on? Explain.

The Ball's in Your Court   Ask the class the following questions:

Do you think it is likely that someone would leap at you if the person was extremely upset with you? What are some ways in which people vent their anger? How do you express anger? Do you think it is best to express anger physically or verbally? Why?

It's Up to You   Present this situation to the students for discussion:

If you had done something to anger or offend another person, what would you say to that person if he began to reprimand you in a loud voice?

Toot Your Own Horn   Have the students compose (orally or in writing) a dialogue or skit based on the following situation:

Imagine that you are in the science lab at school. Your chemistry teacher tells you to prepare certain chemicals for an experiment. In your haste to finish the experiment, you inadvertently knock over some flasks containing expensive chemicals. Your teacher becomes very angry and threatens to report you to the school authorities for your carelessness.

14. Pay Through the Nose

What's Going On?   Ask the class the following questions:

What is the elephant doing? Why? What does he have under his arm? How did he obtain it? Why is the man so happy? Why is he being rewarded?

The Ball's in Your Court   Ask the class the following questions:

What kind of a nose does an elephant have? Is it called a nose? What is a dog's nose called? What are other animals' noses called? In what different ways do we pay for things? Have you ever paid too high a price for something? Under what circumstances? How do you feel if you pay more for something than it is worth?

It's Up to You   Present this situation to the students for discussion:

What would you say you had done if you treated your friends to a high-priced dinner in a luxurious restaurant?

Toot Your Own Horn   Have the students compose (orally or in writing) a dialogue based on the following situation:

For some time now you have been looking for a book written by your favorite author. It is one of his earlier works and has long been out of print. While browsing in a secondhand bookstore one day you happen to come across the book and decide to buy it although it is extremely costly. When you get home, you call a friend and tell her what you did.

15. Tongue-In-Cheek

What's Going On?   Ask the class the following questions:

Why is the man's cheek sticking out? Judging from his facial expression, how would you say he is feeling? Does the man look worried about the comment he just made?

The Ball's in Your Court   Ask the class the following questions:

Under what circumstances would someone take a joking remark seriously? How do you usually feel when someone makes a joking remark about you? Do you know people who always take a joke too seriously? Explain. Do you know people who always take jokes well? Are they more fun to be around? Have you ever had the occasion to make a light-hearted comment to anyone? What was the reaction? Can you make a *tongue-in-cheek* remark about your class or about one of your classmates? Do people need to apologize for joking around with their friends? Do you often make joking remarks when talking with friends?

It's Up to You   Present this situation to the students for discussion:

What kind of remark did the professor make when she told her students that they would not really have to study for the final exam since they would be certain to receive a high grade in the course without studying?

Toot Your Own Horn   Have the students compose (orally or in writing) a dialogue based on the following situation:

Richard and Anna have been friends for a long time. They often talk about contemporary events, sports, and school, and even make jokes about their friends. On their way home from school one day they discuss an incident that occurred in the school cafeteria. Two of their friends had gotten into an argument over a joking, casual remark that one had made to the other about the way he was dressed.

16. Pull Someone's Leg

What's Going On?   Ask the class the following questions:

What type of person is holding the leg in the picture? Why is his hair blowing back? How tall is the person connected to that leg? Do you think the leg belongs to a man or to a woman? Why? What is the man doing with the leg?

The Ball's in Your Court   Ask the class the following questions:

Why would one person want to fool another? Explain a situation in which you fooled someone. Have you ever been deceived by someone else? How do you feel when someone fools you? What is the artist of the picture trying to do by suggesting that someone's leg could be pulled so far?

It's Up to You   Present this situation to the students for discussion:

You know that classes at your school are never held on weekends. What would you say to a person who told you that you missed a special class on pronunciation last Saturday?

Play It by Ear   Have the students compose (orally or in writing) a skit or dialogue based on the following situation:

You happen to run into some friends of yours who have just returned from traveling in a remote area of the world. They describe the things they have seen and done; however, when they talk about certain supernatural occurrences they witnessed and the treasure they brought back with them, you find it impossible to believe them.

17. Play It by Ear

What's Going On?   Ask the class the following questions:

What is the man in the picture doing? Why do you think he is holding the instrument to his ear? What type of instrument is it? How are musical instruments ordinarily played? Does the man seem to be enjoying playing the instrument?

The Ball's in Your Court   Ask the class the following questions:

What is your favorite instrument? Why do you prefer it to other instruments? Name some other instruments and tell how they are played. Can you improvise on an instrument? Are some people better at improvising than others? Can you explain why? When you go out, do you always have definite plans for the entire evening, or do you improvise as you go along? Is it fun to decide what to do as you go along? Do you enjoy not knowing what to expect?

It's Up to You   Present this situation to the students for discussion:

This weekend some relatives that you have not seen for quite some time will be coming to visit you. Since you have not made any definite plans for entertaining them, what will you do during their stay with you?

Toot Your Own Horn   Have the students compose (orally or in writing) a skit or monologue based on the following situation:

You and your friends enjoy attending many school functions such as dances and sporting events. Sometimes you make definite plans for going out after an event, while sometimes you plan to go out but have nothing definite in mind. Describe an occasion when you decided what to do as you went along, and tell how it turned out.

18. Stick Out One's Neck

What's Going On?   Ask the class the following questions:

What is the animal with the long neck called? Is he in any danger of being hurt? Why? Who are the two men hanging on his neck? What type of danger are they in? How could they get hurt? What are the animals in the water called?

The Ball's in Your Court   Ask the class the following questions:

Where do you suppose the men in the picture are? In what position have they placed themselves? Are the animals in the water dangerous? Describe them. What makes them dangerous? Have you ever been in a risky position? Under what circumstances would you take a risk?

It's Up to You   Present this situation to the students for discussion:

Imagine that you were deliberately placing yourself in a position where some harm could come to you. What might a good friend ask you?

Play It by Ear   Have the students compose (orally or in writing) a skit or dialogue based on the following situation:

You and your friend are visiting a big city for the first time. You are amazed by the tall buildings and the stores. Many people are hurrying along the sidewalks, and some are attempting to cross the streets against the signals. Traffic is very heavy. In some sections of the city, new buildings are being constructed and it is dangerous to stand in the vicinity of the construction sites. Describe what you and your friend might do and say.

19. Shake a Leg

What's Going On?   Ask the class the following questions:

Who is the man with the pistol? Why is he firing the gun? Name the animals shown in the picture. What do they have in common? Which one would you say is the slowest? Which one do you think will win the race? Why? What element of humor do you see in the picture?

The Ball's in Your Court   Ask the class the following questions:

Do all animals move about on legs? Can you name some that don't? Do all animals move at the same rate of speed? Name some animals that move slowly and some that move fast. Have you ever been in a competition? If so, what type? What kinds of races can you name? Name some other sports. What are some of the elements necessary for success in any sport? Under what conditions would someone have to hurry? When a person hurries, what does he do with his legs?

It's Up to You   Present this situation to the students for discussion:

If you are late for an appointment and are taking your time about getting ready to go, what is someone likely to tell you?

Play It by Ear   Have the students compose (orally or in writing) a skit based on the following situation:

It's a Saturday afternoon. You were planning to do some shopping, but got tied up with some personal business at home. You need to make some exchanges and buy a birthday gift and an anniversary gift. Unfortunately, the stores close early on Saturdays. You are starting to feel pressured.

20. All Thumbs

What's Going On?   Ask the class the following questions:

What is happening in the picture? Describe the expression on the character's face. How would you say he feels about what he has done? What did he drop? How do you suppose this happened?

The Ball's in Your Court   Ask the class the following questions:

Have you ever dropped or broken something really expensive? Was the accident caused by your clumsiness? What types of situations make you really nervous? How would you characterize a clumsy person? Do clumsy people always hold on to things firmly with both hands? In what ways can a person be clumsy? Do you think that clumsy people are necessarily careless and uncaring?

It's Up to You Present this situation to the students for discussion:

While you were examining a plate at a friend's house, it suddenly slipped out of your hands and broke when it fell to the floor. What type of apology could you offer for what you did?

Toot Your Own Horn Have the students compose (orally or in writing) a dialogue or skit based on the following situation:

Mr. and Mrs. Smith have invited some guests over for a dinner party. The evening starts off with cordial conversation and good food. However, Mrs. Smith becomes very distressed when one of the guests drops her coffee cup. Describe the conversation between Mrs. Smith and her guest.

21. Not Have a Leg to Stand On

What's Going On? Ask the class the following questions:

What is happening to the man in the picture? Why? What is the matter with his legs? What is he wearing on his head? What character or person does he remind you of? What does the man need to keep from falling?

The Ball's in Your Court Ask the class the following questions:

Can you name some circumstances in which people might lose their balance? Have you ever lost your balance? How did it happen? Does a person ordinarily stand on only one leg? If someone has a broken leg, how can he get around? Name some other objects that need legs for support. Describe them. What would happen if a person suddenly twisted his ankle?

It's Up to You Present this situation to the students for discussion:

You have a friend who is a known liar, but who wants people to believe him the next time he wishes to pass on information. What would you tell him?

Toot Your Own Horn Have the students compose (orally or in writing) a dialogue based on the following situation:

A friend of yours is applying for a job as a translator. Although he speaks the foreign language quite well, he has never had any formal training in specialized, technical vocabulary. He's supposed to take an examination in the language to see if he qualifies for the position. He comes to you and tells you about his intentions. What would you say to him?

22. Get Off Someone's Back

What's Going On? Ask the class the following questions:

How does the man feel? How can you tell? How would you describe the creature on his back? What is the creature doing to him? What do you think the man probably wants to do to the creature? Why?

The Ball's in Your Court Ask the class the following questions:

How would you feel if you had something on your back? What would you do if someone wanted to climb on your back? Why? Why do you suppose the creature attached himself to the man in the first place? How would the man feel if he were free of the creature? Do you see any relationship between *being in someone's hair* and *being on someone's back*? Explain. Have you ever bothered someone for something? What prompted you to do so?

It's Up to You   Present this situation to the students for discussion:

If someone were constantly pestering you to go shopping with her and you didn't feel like doing so, what would you tell this person to do?

Play It by Ear   Have the students compose (orally or in writing) a dialogue or skit based on the following situation:

Lately you have been working on a special project that demands a great deal of concentration. Although you have told your roommate not to disturb you for the next several hours, he insists that you look over a composition he has written for his English class.

All's Well That Ends Well

I. Select the best word or phrase to complete each sentence. In some cases, more than one answer is possible.

1. "They got what they wanted, but they had to pay through the nose." "That's for sure. It_____
   _____."
   a. was a bargain
   b. was very costly
   c. was on sale

2. Gosh! I'm all thumbs. I'm so_____I'll never be able to untangle this shoelace.
   a. nervous
   b. clumsy
   c. excited

3. If you insist on pulling his leg every time you see him, he'll never_____
   _____.
   a. believe what you say
   b. let you touch his leg
   c. invite you to his house again

4. "What would you like to do tonight?" "I'm not sure. Let's have dinner, then play it by ear and
   _____."
   a. stay home
   b. see what happens
   c. watch TV

5. Everyone was getting in her hair. She just couldn't get anything done because nobody would
   _____.
   a. leave her alone
   b. help her
   c. stop bothering her

6. He finally got off her back when she told him to_____
   or else she would call the police.
   a. stop annoying her
   b. stop hurting her
   c. stop threatening her

7. You don't have to jump down my throat! I don't_____
   every time you do something wrong.
   a. upset you
   b. contradict you
   c. become angry with you

8. Come on, Ted! Shake a leg or else you'll_____.
   a. miss your plane
   b. be there early
   c. not be late

THE BODY HAS MANY USES **23**

9. He's always shooting off his mouth about something, but_____
   what he says.
   a. he's always quiet about
   b. nobody believes
   c. everybody likes

10. It was just a tongue-in-cheek remark. She wasn't really_____.
    a. serious
    b. joking
    c. angry

11. By sticking your neck out for Jack you_____.
    Everyone knows he can't be trusted.
    a. don't have to worry
    b. are taking a great risk
    c. might get in the way

12. _____they didn't have a leg to stand on.
    a. When all the facts were known,
    b. When they got tired,
    c. When they were caught spying,

II. Complete the sentences in the following dialogues with idioms from the list below. Make changes in grammar and wording where needed.

get in someone's hair   shoot off one's mouth
jump down someone's throat   pay through the nose
tongue-in-cheek   pull someone's leg
play it by ear   stick out one's neck
shake a leg   all thumbs
not have a leg to stand on   get off someone's back

Dialogue 1

John: Don't tell me you meant all those bad things you said about Joe!

Roger: Of course not! I was just_____. You know I wasn't serious.
                                  (kidding you)

John: I thought it might be a_____remark, but I wasn't sure.
                                (not very serious)

Roger: Well, you know Joe. He's always_____about
                              (loudly proclaiming to one and all)

how hard he has to work. I guess I was upset when I heard him telling everybody

to_____, since I work just as hard!
                    (stop bothering him)

Dialogue 2

Susan: I'm not going to_____for you any longer. With
                      (place myself at risk)

all those lies you told, I won't_____if I try to
                            (have any defense)

convince them to believe you.

Lois: Well, why don't you_____when they ask if you had any
                 (make something up as you go along)

knowledge of what I did?

Susan: Sure, and then they'll_____when they find out that
                 (become very angry with me)

I tried to keep the truth from them. I know that if I try to cover up for you I'll

_____.
              (pay a very high price)

Dialogue 3

Peter: Hey, Paul. You'd better_____. I'm not going to wait for
(hurry up)

you any longer!

Paul: Just wait a minute! Can't you see that I'm not dressed yet? These buttons on my shirt are

really hard to do up and I'm_____! I'm so
(very clumsy at what I'm doing)

nervous I can't think straight!

Peter: I'm sorry. I didn't mean to_____about getting
(annoy you and make you angry)

ready. It's just that we're already late and the girls will think we aren't coming.

III. Fill in the blanks below, then find and circle the missing words in the puzzle. Be sure to look horizontally, vertically, and diagonally.

1. bother someone: get in someone's_____

2. become angry with someone: jump down someone's_____

3. not serious: _____-in-cheek

4. improvise as one goes along: play it by_____

5. hurry: _____a leg

6. to have no good defense for one's opinions or actions: not have a_____to stand on

7. stop bothering someone: get off someone's_____

8. clumsy: all_____

9. take a risk: stick out one's_____

10. fool someone: _____someone's leg

11. pay too high a price: pay through the_____

12. express one's own opinions loudly: shoot off one's_____

n	e	c	k	z	b	l	r	h	b	n	h	k	h	l	b	t	s	m	o	q	u	l	x	r	b
h	q	y	l	x	a	t	y	c	d	m	t	n	r	x	l	t	w	a	s	p	r	o	a	y	x
k	j	o	a	t	u	c	t	l	e	a	u	n	b	l	p	s	k	j	t	q	i	e	r	h	b
r	y	n	c	j	h	e	n	a	k	e	o	r	c	l	i	m	r	a	s	l	o	e	g	i	c
s	n	u	f	l	w	r	b	d	n	s	m	m	n	i	o	l	s	n	e	e	i	e	a	k	i
j	d	v	g	n	y	g	o	d	t	m	t	y	e	n	s	o	n	i	n	j	h	o	i	m	a
i	e	w	p	p	a	i	f	a	k	a	h	l	h	a	i	r	e	a	e	j	l	p	n	e	t
e	p	f	u	l	d	r	y	p	t	h	u	m	b	s	c	a	e	l	o	a	g	l	n	b	y
a	l	g	l	r	r	y	n	k	e	s	t	o	m	y	l	o	s	h	y	n	e	m	i	s	i
l	m	p	l	t	y	s	a	r	t	b	x	i	q	o	l	r	n	c	y	h	l	j	c	k	e
b	a	r	h	s	l	t	o	g	e	c	k	g	r	o	p	t	l	l	c	d	c	b	r	i	t
m	n	l	i	q	b	j	v	b	t	a	h	d	x	v	e	o	i	o	v	e	l	e	s	m	y
y	k	s	h	a	k	e	n	d	s	l	k	h	i	s	k	n	s	l	r	b	y	n	t	c	y
c	r	y	k	o	z	h	q	f	t	a	o	j	h	f	o	g	c	h	d	n	d	f	x	c	t
k	b	q	e	m	x	f	c	u	w	u	n	r	l	d	v	u	u	l	k	s	n	o	s	e	k
t	h	f	d	k	v	d	j	a	b	d	c	x	t	f	y	e	p	d	j	x	v	h	e	y	o
o	s	j	b	b	a	c	k	k	n	m	q	j	l	n	m	k	r	o	n	s	c	o	b	j	m

Answer Key

I. 1. b   5. a or c   9. b (or c)
    2. b   6. a   10. a
    3. a   7. c   11. b
    4. b   8. a   12. a or c

II. **Dialogue 1**

pulling your leg, tongue-in-cheek, shooting off his mouth, get off his back (or get out of his hair)

Dialogue 2

stick my neck out, have a leg to stand on, play it by ear, jump down my throat, pay through the nose

Dialogue 3

shake a leg, all thumbs, get in your hair (or get on your back)

III. 1. hair   5. shake   9. neck
     2. throat   6. leg   10. pull
     3. tongue   7. back   11. nose
     4. ear   8. thumbs   12. mouth

```
n  e  c  k  z  b  l  r  h  b  n  h  k  h  l  b  t  s  m  o  q  u  l  x  r  b
h  q  y  l  x  a  t  y  c  d  m  t  n  r  x  l  t  w  a  s  p  r  o  a  y  x
k  j  o  a  t  u  c  t  l  e  a  u  n  b  l  p  s  k  j  t  q  i  e  r  h  b
r  y  n  c  j  h  e  n  a  k  e  o  r  c  l  i  m  r  a  s  l  o  e  g  i  c
s  n  u  f  l  w  r  b  d  n  s  m  m  n  i  o  l  s  n  e  e  i  e  a  k  i
j  d  v  g  n  y  g  o  d  t  m  t  y  e  n  s  o  n  i  n  j  h  o  i  m  a
i  e  w  p  p  a  i  f  a  k  a  h  l  h  a  i  r  e  a  e  j  l  p  n  e  t
e  p  f  u  l  d  r  y  p  t  h  u  m  b  s  c  a  e  l  o  a  g  l  n  b  y
a  l  g  l  r  r  y  n  k  e  s  t  o  m  y  l  o  s  h  y  n  e  m  i  s  i
l  m  p  l  t  y  s  a  r  b  x  i  q  o  l  r  n  c  y  h  l  j  c  k  e
b  a  r  h  s  l  t  o  g  e  c  k  g  r  o  p  t  l  l  c  d  c  b  r  i  t
m  n  l  i  q  b  j  v  b  t  a  h  d  x  v  e  o  i  o  v  e  l  e  s  m  y
y  k  s  h  a  k  e  n  d  s  l  k  h  i  s  k  n  s  l  r  b  y  n  t  c  y
c  r  y  k  o  z  h  q  f  t  a  o  j  h  f  o  g  c  h  d  n  d  f  x  c  t
k  b  q  e  m  x  f  c  u  w  u  n  r  l  d  v  u  u  l  k  s  n  o  s  e  k
t  h  f  d  k  v  d  j  a  b  d  c  x  t  f  y  e  p  d  j  x  v  h  e  y  o
o  s  j  b  b  a  c  k  k  n  m  q  j  l  n  m  k  r  o  n  s  c  o  b  j  m
```

Section Three

That's Not Nice

23. Drive Someone Up a Wall

What's Going On?   Ask the class the following questions:

Why do you think one of the men is walking up the wall? How do you think he feels? How can you tell? What seems to be bothering him? Why do you think he wants to try to walk up a wall? What instrument is the other man playing? How is he playing the instrument? What is he using to play the instrument? Does he seem to care what other people think of his playing? Is he enjoying what he's doing?

The Ball's in Your Court   Ask the class the following questions:

What do you do when you want to get away from a situation that bothers you? Describe some situations that you might want to get away from. Do you get annoyed when you hear loud music? What do you feel like doing when you're annoyed? Think of another idiom that indicates annoyance. How are these two idioms related? In what way(s) are they different?

It's Up to You   Present this situation to the students for discussion:

If someone were doing something that made you very angry, how would you tell this person about the effect his actions were having on you?

Toot Your Own Horn   Have the students compose (orally or in writing) a skit or dialogue based on the following situation:

Imagine that you are the director of a social club. You always do your best to arrange activities that the members will like. However, some of the members never seem to be satisfied. They are constantly complaining and saying that they could do better. One of the members in particular has been greatly annoying you lately. You are tired of listening to him.

24. String Someone Along

What's Going On?   Ask the class the following questions:

What is the man dangling in front of the woman? Why? Judging from the expression on his face, what would you say his intentions are? Is he being honest with the woman? In your opinion, why is the woman running? Does she seem more interested in the man or in what he is offering her? Do you think that the man will eventually give her the necklace?

The Ball's in Your Court   Ask the class the following questions:

Has anyone ever made you a promise and later broken it? What made you believe what the person said in the first place? Have you ever been disappointed or deceived? Can you think of any synonyms for *deceit*? Why do you think anyone would ever want to deceive another person? Can you think of any situation in which deceit or a lie might be justified? Have your friends always been sincere with you? If not, have you ever thought they were taking advantage of you?

It's Up to You   Present this situation to the students for discussion:

If someone was deceiving you and leading you on under false pretenses, what would this person be doing to you?

Toot Your Own Horn
Have the students compose (orally or in writing) a skit or dialogue based on the following situation:

Alicia has been your friend since childhood and has always confided in you. Lately she has been going out with a man who says he loves her and has bought her a number of gifts. Nevertheless, he refuses to make any commitment for a lasting relationship. You discuss the matter with Alicia and tell her what you think.

25. Sell Someone Down the River

What's Going On?
Ask the class the following questions:

What are the three people sitting in? How does the man in the boat feel? Why? What does the woman who is standing have in her hands? What is she doing? What is she wearing? Is she happy or sad? Explain. What do you think has just happened? Where would you say that this scene is taking place? What makes you think so?

The Ball's in Your Court
Ask the class the following questions:

Have you ever confided in anyone? If so, explain the circumstances. Did that person keep your confidence? If not, how did you feel? What did you do? Can you name other vessels of the sea? Can you think of any situation in which someone might betray a friend for personal gain? Can you think of other reasons why a person might betray a friend? In your mind, is there any possible justification for such a betrayal?

It's Up to You
Present this situation to the students for discussion:

Richard confided some personal information to a friend of his. His friend then revealed the information to someone else for a large sum of money. Describe what Richard's friend did to him.

Play It by Ear
Have the students compose (orally or in writing) a skit or dialogue based on the following situation:

A group of thieves stole a number of valuable paintings from an art gallery. They were successful in selling the paintings, but then they started to argue over how the money would be distributed. One of the members of the gang was very dissatisfied with his share of the money and went to the police. They promised him immunity from prosecution for revealing the names of the gang members and telling them where the paintings had been sold. Describe the conversation between the gang member and the police.

26. Leave Someone High and Dry

What's Going On?
Ask the class the following questions:

Where is this scene taking place? What is growing there? What is the weather like? Are there many people around? Why not? Why do you suppose the giraffes are looking at the ground? Do you think they are thirsty? Do you think the location shown in the picture is a likely place for giraffes to be found? Where are giraffes usually found?

The Ball's in Your Court
Ask the class the following questions:

Name some animals that are usually found in hot, dry places. Do they need much water to live? How would you feel if you were all alone in the middle of a desolate area? Have you ever been abandoned? If so, describe the situation. Can you think of different ways in which people can be left all alone? What would you think of someone who was helping you with a project and then left suddenly?

It's Up to You   Present this situation to the students for discussion:

Mrs. Green's husband ran off and left her with three children to raise all by herself. How would you describe what Mr. Green did to his wife?

Play It by Ear   Have the students compose (orally or in writing) an essay or skit based on the following situation:

Imagine that you are on an expedition in the jungles of the Amazon region. You have hired some native guides who speak several of the Indian dialects. So far you have had a rewarding experience. However, one day while walking through some thick underbrush, your guides see some human skulls and become frightened. When you wake up the next morning, you find that you are all alone. The guides have fled. What will you do?

27. Sell Someone Short

What's Going On?   Ask the class the following questions:

What is the man carrying? Why? Why do you suppose people are passing him by? How do you think he feels? Do you think he is inferior to other people? If so, in what way? In what way(s) is he the same as other people?

The Ball's in Your Court   Ask the class the following questions:

When someone is not the same as everyone else, what do people tend to think of him? Do you think this opinion is justified? What do you suppose that "someone different" thinks of himself? Has anyone ever underestimated you? If so, how did you react? Do you always give people the credit they deserve? If you don't, why not?

It's Up to You   Present this situation to the students for discussion:

John has a physical handicap, but in spite of his handicap he has always excelled at sports. Most people are aware of his handicap but are not aware of his athletic abilities. As a result, what do you think they have a tendency to do?

Play It by Ear   Have the students compose (orally or in writing) a skit or dialogue based on the following situation:

Joe was always poor in math. Nevertheless, he was a hard worker and had a keen desire to succeed. He finished school as an average student and began working in a department store. At nights he would work for hours on various inventions. He was certain that one day he would be able to start his own company, but nobody would believe him. Needless to say, he eventually became a very successful businessman. One day Joe met and talked with one of his old neighbors.

28. Snow Job

What's Going On?   Ask the class the following questions:

How is the tall man speaking? Does the other man seem interested in what he is saying? Why do you suppose the tall man is so animated? Why do you think one of the men is dressed in winter clothing and the other is not? What do you suppose the tall man is trying to do? How is the short man reacting? In view of how the short man is dressed, what do you think the little white specks represent?

The Ball's in Your Court   Ask the class the following questions:

How do people ordinarily dress for winter weather? Name some articles of clothing that are worn in the winter. What does snow do to the buildings, trees, and ground? Has anybody ever tried to convince you that something was true by covering up the real facts about the situation? If so, describe what happened. If a person tried to convince you of something by talking in an animated, exaggerated manner, would you believe him? Would you have any reason not to?

It's Up to You   Present this situation to the students for discussion:

If someone tried to convince you to buy goods you knew were of poor craftsmanship and quality, what would you say that person was doing to you?

Toot Your Own Horn   Have the students compose (orally or in writing) a dialogue based on the following situation:

Imagine that a friend of yours wanted to buy a used car. He went out looking and came home exhausted and frustrated. He calls you on the phone and tells you about his experiences with some of the car dealers. Basically, he has found that they exaggerate the merits of their cars and that they try to convince you to buy something that is clearly not worth the money.

29. Spill the Beans

What's Going On?   Ask the class the following questions:

Why do you think the people in the picture are pointing at each other? Under what circumstances would anyone want to point at another person? Would it necessarily be to accuse that person of wrongdoing? What is lying on the floor in the picture? What connection do you see between what's on the floor and what the people are doing?

The Ball's in Your Court   Ask the class the following questions:

Has anyone ever pointed a finger at you? If so, what was the reason? Have you ever been falsely accused? If so, how did you react? What are some reasons why someone might point a finger at another person? Can you tell what a box or bag contains if it does not have a label? Why would a person want to know the contents of a sealed container? What similarities can you see between *letting the cat out of the bag* and *spilling the beans*? Have you ever told anybody about a forthcoming event that was supposed to be kept a secret? What happened when it became known that you had revealed private information?

It's Up to You   Present this situation to the students for discussion:

After attending a confidential meeting, William told another person what had happened behind closed doors. What could one say about William?

Play It by Ear   Have the students compose (orally or in writing) a skit or dialogue based on the following situation:

Mr. and Mrs. Thomas had been planning a surprise trip to the West Coast to visit their daughter Natalie, whom they had not seen for two years. They kept their intended trip a secret from everyone except a close friend of Natalie's. Unfortunately, while speaking with Natalie one day, the friend let slip the information that her parents were going to drop in on her unexpectedly.

30. Feed Someone a Line

What's Going On?   Ask the class the following questions:

Where is the man sitting? What type of hat is he wearing? What is he holding in his hands? What's tied to the end of the fishing pole? What does the note say? Does the man appear to be sincere? Does he know the person under the water? Who is under the water? What is her reaction to the note?

The Ball's in Your Court   Ask the class the following questions:

Is it hard or easy to tell if someone is trying to deceive you? Explain. Name some ways in which one person might try to deceive another. Has anybody ever led you along with false promises? Do you see any similarities between *stringing someone along* and *feeding someone a line*? Under what circumstances might these idioms be used?

It's Up to You   Present this situation to the students for discussion:

If someone of modest means promised to take you on an extended trip around the world, what would you think?

Toot Your Own Horn   Have the students compose (orally or in writing) a skit or dialogue based on the following situation:

Alberto and Sonia are very good friends of yours. Sonia has often spoken to you about her desire to visit Europe. Some time ago Alberto came home and told Sonia that he had gotten a promotion at work and a good raise in salary. He led his wife to believe that they would be departing for Europe during the Easter holidays. Now Easter has passed and Alberto has not made good on his promise. Sonia is expressing her disappointment to you.

All's Well That Ends Well

I. Complete the sentences with idioms from the list below. Make changes in grammar and wording where needed.

drive someone up a wall	string someone along
sell someone down the river	leave someone high and dry
sell someone short	snow job
spill the beans	feed someone a line

1. Be careful! Don't_____! The fact that he doesn't say much doesn't mean he doesn't know what's going on every step of the way.

2. OK! That's it! No more! You're_____ with all that screaming and hollering! Why don't you all go outside and play?

3. I don't know who_____, but I'll tell you one thing: whoever told Lynne and John what I was planning is going to pay dearly for opening his big mouth!

4. It's not hard to understand why she_____. He had constantly mistreated her. It was only natural that she would want to get away from it all.

5. There was no reason for that guy to give us a_____about the merits of that racing bike. He knew from the beginning that we had no intention of buying.

6. Don't_____about how good you are on the tennis court! I've seen you play, and I know I can beat you any time!

7. You know, I don't appreciate what you did. You were just_____ _____when you said I'd get that promotion. At least you could have been honest with me so I could have taken another job.

8. Go ahead!_____! Tell them whatever you want! By the time they come knocking on my door, I'll be long gone!

© National Textbook Company **THAT'S NOT NICE** **37**

II. Match the situation in column A with the idiom in column B.

A

_____ 1. Look. Don't go making any promises you don't intend to keep.

_____ 2. I never expected him to make such astonishing progress.

_____ 3. Her boss expected her to work long hours for low pay, and he rarely spoke to her except to complain.

_____ 4. Why weren't those two men thrown into prison with all the rest?

_____ 5. Annette finds it hard to believe that any man can be sincere. Look how many times she's been deceived!

_____ 6. He wasn't at all surprised when the committee informed him he had won first prize in the literary contest.

_____ 7. Why did they ever buy such an ugly-looking car?

_____ 8. I'm not surprised that Mr. Jones decided to quit teaching music. He couldn't take listening to all those kids play out of tune!

B

a. I have no idea. Someone must have given them a pretty good snow job.

b. Come on, now. Do you really think I'd try to string you along?

c. Of course. This isn't the first time someone has fed her a line.

d. See? I warned you not to sell him short!

e. They sold the other members of their gang down the river, and in return the authorities promised them immunity from prosecution.

f. I know. All that awful playing was driving him up a wall.

g. Why not? Did somebody spill the beans?

h. It didn't surprise anyone when she took another job and left him high and dry.

III. Complete the crossword puzzle using the clues below. (The idioms in the puzzle are from sections two and three.)

Across

2. get in someone's_____

7. play it by_____

8. _____someone along

9. stick out one's_____

10. all_____

12. spill the_____

14. tongue-in-_____

15. leave someone high and_____

Down

1. sell someone_____

3. sell someone down the_____

4. jump down someone's_____

5. feed someone a_____

6. _____someone up a wall

8. _____a leg

9. pay through the_____

11. shoot off one's_____

12. get off someone's_____

13. not have a leg to_____on

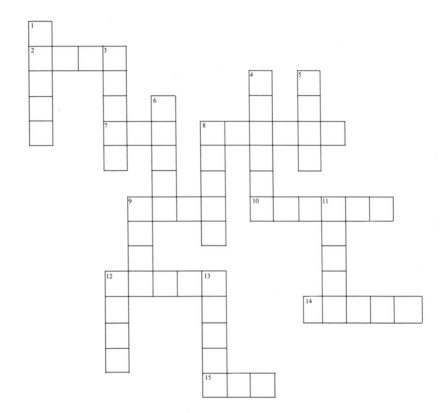

Answer Key

I. 1. sell him short
    2. driving me up the wall
    3. spilled the beans
    4. left him high and dry

    5. snow job
    6. feed me a line
    7. stringing me along
    8. Sell me down the river

II. 1. b
    2. d
    3. h

    4. e
    5. c
    6. g

    7. a
    8. f

III.

Section Four

People Do the Strangest Things

31. On Ice

What's Going On? Ask the class the following questions:

Why do you think the books are lying on top of a block of ice? Why do you suppose the Eskimos put them there? What do you think will happen to the books? What are the two Eskimos holding? What are they doing? Do they look happy? Why do you think so?

The Ball's in Your Court Ask the class the following questions:

What is the purpose of freezing something or putting it "on ice"? Where do Eskimos live? Describe the clothing that Eskimos wear. Where does it come from? What is a traditional Eskimo house called? What is it made of? Do you know how Eskimos keep their igloos warm? What food do Eskimos eat a lot of? Have you ever set any project aside temporarily? Under what circumstances?

It's Up to You Present this situation to the students for discussion:

If you got tired of doing your homework and wanted to set it aside for a little while, what would you say?

Play It by Ear Have the students compose (orally or in writing) a skit or dialogue based on the following situation:

Pretend that you are an architect working on the design for a new shopping center. After many months of work you feel that you have run out of ideas. You decide that it's time to take a break and get back to the project in a week or so. You go to your supervisor to explain your decision and hear her reaction.

32. Shoot the Breeze

What's Going On? Ask the class the following questions:

What is the man shooting at? What's he shooting with? What is the weather like? Are the bullets having any effect? Why not? What sound do you hear when you fire a gun? Would you say that the man is engaging in a serious activity? How does he feel about what he is doing? How can you tell?

The Ball's in your Court Ask the class the following questions:

Describe the general atmosphere of a party or a social gathering. What do people talk about at informal gatherings? What do you talk about when you bump into an old friend you have not seen for a long time? Describe a formal occasion. How do formal occasions differ from informal gatherings? What do people talk about at formal gatherings? Do you see any connection between the man shooting aimlessly into the air and an informal, unplanned conversation? Is there a common factor?

It's Up to You Present this situation to the students for discussion:

A friend you have not seen for a long time invites you to sit and chat about old times over a cup of coffee. How would you describe your conversation?

Toot Your Own Horn Have the students compose (orally or in writing) a dialogue or skit based on the following situation:

A group of dignitaries has gathered for a series of formal talks concerning the strengthening of political ties, trade, and cultural exchanges between their nations. Although the talks are of a serious nature, the dignitaries do occasionally take time off from their meetings to chat on an informal basis. Create a dialogue that illustrates both a formal and an informal encounter between the dignitaries.

33. Bite the Dust

What's Going On?   Ask the class the following questions:

How is the man buried in the sandpile? What was he trying to do? How do you imagine he got into this position? In what type of sport was he engaged? How is he dressed? What does his clothing suggest to you? Would you say that he was successful in his endeavor?

The Ball's in Your Court   Ask the class the following questions:

What are some of your favorite sports? Are you good at any of them? Name some sports that require a team of players and some sports that are played on an individual basis. How do players feel when they win? How do they feel when they lose? Have you ever been in a competition? If so, describe it. How did you do?

It's Up to You   Present this situation to the students for discussion:

If you were a spectator at a boxing match, what would you say about the guy who got knocked out?

Toot Your Own Horn   Have the students compose (orally or in writing) a skit or dialogue based on the following situation:

The twelfth international sports competition is taking place in your city. Many tourists have arrived from all parts of the world to witness the competitions. They discuss the various events and talk about the victories and defeats of both the teams and the individual players. Create a conversation between some tourists about the recent basketball and tennis competitions.

34. Bend Over Backwards

What's Going On?   Ask the class the following questions:

Are the two people leaning over backwards uncomfortable? Why? Judging from their facial expressions, what would you say about them? Describe the woman who is walking over them. Judging from her expression, do you think she feels badly about what she's doing? Do you think the man and woman leaning over backwards are supporting her in some way? If so, how?

The Ball's in Your Court   Ask the class the following questions:

Is it hard or easy to bend over backwards? Have you ever tried very hard to help someone out? If so, what was the occasion? What did you do? How did the other person benefit from your efforts? Name some different ways in which people can help others out. Has anyone ever made a great effort to help you out of a tight spot? If so, describe the occasion.

It's Up to You   Present this situation to the students for discussion:

You have just started a new job and it is difficult to remember everything that has to be done before leaving the office. Your new coworkers go out of their way to help you whenever you have any trouble with the routine. What would you say about your fellow workers?

Play It by Ear   Have the students compose (orally or in writing) an essay or monologue based on the following situation:

The students in your class are having an end-of-the-year social gathering. You are in charge of the food and entertainment. There are two or three other people on your committee who are hard workers and have volunteered to help you out. You all work very hard and the affair is a great success. You are very thankful to the members of your committee for their help and support. Describe the affair and the contributions that everyone made toward its success.

35. Hit the Hay

What's Going On?   Ask the class the following questions:

How is the man feeling? How can you tell? What position is he in? What is he getting ready to do? Where will he land? How is he dressed? What will he do when he hits the hay?

The Ball's in Your Court   Ask the class the following questions:

Where is hay usually found? What is it primarily used for? What are some other uses for hay? What do people do when they are sleepy? On what do they usually sleep? Name some other things on which people sometimes sleep. What items do we use for making a bed? Do you think it is necessary to sleep eight hours every night? Why or why not? What things can make a person sleepy? If a person is sleepy, what can he do to keep awake? Have you ever fallen asleep in class or during an important event? If so, describe the situation. What did you do to try to keep awake?

It's Up to You   Present this situation to the students for discussion:

If you were very sleepy and wanted to go to bed right away, what would you say to your family?

Play It by Ear   Have the students compose (orally or in writing) a dialogue based on the following situation:

This has been a very busy week. You have been staying up very late making final preparations for your daughter's wedding. You have been running around doing last-minute shopping and talking with the florist and photographer. Describe your routine and sleeping habits to a friend.

36. Cough Up

What's Going On?   Ask the class the following questions:

What is the man on the left doing to the other man? Why is he doing this? What does he expect? Describe the man who is bending over. What is he doing? Is he happy about what he's doing? What does his facial expression indicate?

The Ball's in Your Court   Ask the class the following questions:

Have you ever had to give something up unwillingly? If so, how did you act when you did so? Is it difficult to get someone to say or do something that he does not want to do? How might you go about persuading someone to give something up? Why might one person try to get something from someone else? Would it be for personal benefit? Name some things that might cause a person to cough. What might cause a person to sneeze?

It's Up to You   Present this situation to the students for discussion:

If someone owed you money and refused to pay you back, even though he had the money to do so, what could you say to get him to give you the money?

Toot Your Own Horn   Have the students compose (orally or in writing) a skit or dialogue based on the following situation:

Jim, William, and Richard are good friends and enjoy going out together to a movie or to a basketball or football game. Richard, however, is somewhat conservative with his money. When Jim or William uses his own money to buy tickets for everyone, Richard seldom offers to pay back his share of the cost of the tickets. Unfortunately, his friends often have to ask him to pay what he owes.

37. Jump the Gun

What's Going On?   Ask the class the following questions:

What was the man trying to do? Was he successful? Why or why not? Why do you think he was jumping over the cannon? Do you suppose he was in a hurry? What should he have done to avoid getting hit by the cannonball?

The Ball's in Your Court   Ask the class the following questions:

Name some weapons other than cannons. What do all these weapons have in common? What are they used for? Do you see any relationship between the motion of an object fired from a gun and the actions of someone who is pressed for time? Have you ever been so excited about something that you just couldn't wait to tell someone about it? If so, describe the situation. Have you ever done something before you were supposed to? What was the outcome? When people do something in haste, do you think they are often sorry? Why? Has anyone ever ruined a surprise for you by being hasty and revealing some news too soon? If so, how did you react?

It's Up to You   Present this situation to the students for discussion:

A friend of yours was supposed to register for school on August 25; however, he showed up for registration on August 24. What would you say he did?

Play It by Ear   Have the students compose (orally or in writing) a skit or dialogue based on the following situation:

Mrs. Ramsey is a professor of English. She has a class of intermediate students and has been explaining some points of grammar to them. While illustrating the usage of the past tense, she inadvertently began talking about compound tenses and other more advanced structures. A student makes the point that the class has not yet reached this level in the language. The professor admits that she was getting ahead of herself.

38. Scratch Someone's Back

What's Going On?   Ask the class the following questions:

What reason could the man and woman have for scratching each other's backs? Could it be because of any physical discomfort? Judging from their facial expressions, how would you say they feel about what's going on? What are they using to scratch each other's backs? Can you tell whether the two people started scratching at the same time, or whether one of them initiated the action? Do you think they are helping each other out in some way?

The Ball's in Your Court   Ask the class the following questions:

Can you scratch your own back? Why not? What makes a person want to scratch his or her back? What effect does scratching the back have? How would you feel about helping someone out if he helped you out in some way? Would you simply feel obligated, or would you really want to return the favor? Explain. Has anyone ever done you a big favor? What did you do to reciprocate?

It's Up to You   Present this situation to the students for discussion:

Imagine that you are having a problem with something and a friend offers to help you out. What might you say to indicate that you'd be willing to return the favor?

Toot Your Own Horn   Have the students compose (orally or in writing) a dialogue or skit based on the following situation:

Carlos and Anita are students at the university. Before graduating, they each must pass examinations in math and English. They are talking at the student union. Carlos, who is very good in math, talks about his plans to become an engineer. Anita plans to become an English teacher. Although she does very well in English, she lets Carlos know that she is having trouble with her math courses. At this point, Carlos admits that he has been having problems with his English. The two become good friends and agree to help each other.

39. Hit the Ceiling

What's Going On?   Ask the class the following questions:

What is the man doing? How do you think the man is feeling? What happened to the man's head? What did he hit? How do you think he felt when he hit his head? Do you think the man is upset? What could have happened to make him feel that way?

The Ball's in Your Court   Ask the class the following questions:

How do you react when you get very angry? Do you hit things? Have you ever felt like hitting your head against something? What made you feel that way? Describe some different ways a person might express anger. When a person is very angry, is he in a good position to control or "put a ceiling" on his anger? Name some different things that make people angry.

It's Up to You   Present this situation to the students for discussion:

Imagine that you came home and found that your apartment had been robbed and that the thieves had made off with some of your most valuable possessions. What would you do?

Play It by Ear   Have the students compose (orally or in writing) a skit or dialogue based on the following situation:

Mr. Thomas is the manager of a large supermarket. He is responsible for the correct pricing of all items sold in the store. He meets regularly with the stock boys and gives them the latest price sheets so they can keep the prices of the goods up to date. One day, one of the stock boys accidentally picked up an old price list and thus mismarked hundreds of items. When Mr. Thomas noticed the erroneous prices, he became very angry and resolved to have a talk with the stock boys.

40. Fork Over

What's Going On?   Ask the class the following questions:

What is the man holding in his hand? What is he doing with the fork? Do you think the man is trying to feed someone? What is he handing over? Does he appear to be happy about what he's doing? Do you think he is doing it willingly?

The Ball's in Your Court   Ask the class the following questions:

Have you ever had to give something up unwillingly? Was the person who demanded it justified in doing so? Have you ever owed anyone any money? How did you feel about having to pay it back? Do you see a similarity between *cough up* and *fork over*?

It's Up to You   Present this situation to the students for discussion:

Someone has taken a book of yours that you need. This person refuses to give it back to you when you ask for it. How could you ask for the return of your book in an insistent manner?

Toot Your Own Horn   Have the students compose (orally or in writing) a skit based on the following situation:

A group of boys at school are discussing a prank they wish to play on Ed. They know that it is his sixteenth birthday and that Helen has invited him out for a hamburger and a Coke this afternoon. While Ed is in the shower after gym class, his friends hide his pants, socks, and shoes. Ed suspects that his friends are playing a joke on him since it is his birthday. He confronts his pals in the locker room and insists that they return his clothes.

41. Turn Someone Off

What's Going On?   Ask the class the following questions:

What does the woman have on her back? What is it used for? In what position is the switch? How do you think the woman is feeling? Do you think that the woman would feel better if the switch were in the "on" position? What makes you think so?

The Ball's in Your Court   Ask the class the following questions:

Under what circumstances can an electrical appliance function? Does it have to be plugged into an electrical outlet? Does the switch have to be in the "on" position? Name and describe several different electrical appliances and tell how they are used. How do you suppose a person would feel if he could not renew his energy? How would you feel toward a person who deprived you of your energy? Has anyone ever said or done anything that was very distasteful to you? If so, describe the occasion. Do you think the same things annoy all people? Give some examples to support your answer. What are some of your "pet peeves"?

It's Up to You   Present this situation to the students for discussion:

You have always been a neat, orderly person. Disorganized, untidy people repel you. How would you express your aversion to someone who was careless about his appearance or personal grooming?

Play It by Ear   Have the students compose (orally or in writing) a dialogue or skit based on the following situation:

Gina and Henry have known each other for quite some time. Gina has always refused to spend any time with Henry because he is so ill-mannered. On the few occasions when they have been at the same social function, Gina has always made an excuse to leave early. Poor Henry simply can't understand why Gina is so curt with him. One day he finds a chance to ask her about her behavior toward him.

42. Go Fly a Kite

What's Going On?   Ask the class the following questions:

What is the man holding? How does he feel about what he is doing? How can you tell? In what direction is the kite going? What helps to keep a kite up in the air? What would happen if the man were to let go of the string?

The Ball's in Your Court   Ask the class the following questions:

What type of activity is "flying a kite"? Define the word *pastime* and name some other pastimes. Has anyone ever asked you to leave him or her alone? Why would anyone want to be left alone? Have you ever done something that has greatly annoyed another person? If so, describe the occasion. What are some things that might bother people? Has anyone ever "gotten in your hair"? If so, how have you reacted?

It's Up to You   Present this situation to the students for discussion:

If a person is constantly bothering you, what could you say to make him go away and leave you alone?

Toot Your Own Horn   Have the students compose (orally or in writing) a skit or dialogue based on the following situation:

Jack and Lorraine are discussing a gift they have to buy for a friend's wedding. Joe keeps interrupting them with wisecracks about marriage while they are trying to make a decision. After a while, Jack and Lorraine become greatly irritated with Joe. They want to be left alone.

43. Kick the Bucket

What's Going On?   Ask the class the following questions:

In what position is the old man lying? What do you think he is doing in this position? What is on the man's left foot? Does this have anything to do with what happened to the man? Can he tell us how he got into this position? Why not?

The Ball's in Your Court Ask the class the following questions:

When someone is in a prone position, is he necessarily sleeping? For what other reason(s) might somebody be lying down? If you were standing on a bucket and someone kicked it out from under you, what would happen to you? Is it possible to get seriously hurt by falling? Explain your answer. What do you think would happen to a person who fell from any type of support and hit his head on a sharp, pointed object? Could this result in a fatal injury?

It's Up to You Present this situation to the students for discussion:

If you wanted to describe a person's death in an informal, somewhat impolite manner, what could you say?

Play It by Ear Have the students compose (orally or in writing) a skit based on the following situation:

Old Mr. Jackson lived by himself on the outskirts of town. He had a reputation for being eccentric. At times people would see him in his garden or at the store, buying supplies. He seemed to be in fairly good health. However, one day a neighbor realizes she hasn't seen Mr. Jackson for some time. She checks with several other neighbors and shopkeepers, and finds that he has not been seen for the past two weeks. The authorities investigate.

44. Raise a Stink

What's Going On? Ask the class the following questions:

What kind of animals are shown in the illustration? How do skunks protect themselves? What is the "lady" doing? What is the reaction of the "man"? Would you say he approves of her actions? Why do you think so? How does the lady feel about herself?

The Ball's in Your Court Ask the class the following questions:

In what ways can people show dissatisfaction or disapproval? Have you ever done or said anything that has brought about disapproval? If so, describe the occasion. When one person shows strong dissatisfaction with another person's actions or behavior, how might the latter react? Name some other small animals and tell how they protect themselves. Have you ever had reason to make a fuss about something? If so, describe the circumstances. Has anyone ever made a fuss about anything you've said or done?

It's Up to You Present this situation to the students for discussion:

If you were mistreated as a customer of a store, in what way could you make your feelings known to the manager?

Toot Your Own Horn Have the students compose (orally or in writing) a skit based on the following situation:

The planning commission has decided to tear down some old buildings near your home. Plans are underway to build a freeway in the area. Many children live and play in the area. You are one of many citizens who are extremely dissatisfied with this decision and who plan to lodge a protest with the city authorities.

All's Well That Ends Well

I. Select the best idiom to complete each sentence. In some cases, more than one answer is possible.

1. Since Dan owed them so much, he was hesitant to_____.
   a. cough up the money
   b. bite the dust
   c. fork over any cash

2. There's nothing the Jacksons won't do for their guests. They'd_____
   _____to please them.
   a. go fly a kite
   b. bend over backwards
   c. scratch their backs

3. None of the kids felt like going anyplace. They all wanted to sit around and_____
   _____.
   a. raise a stink
   b. put everything on ice
   c. shoot the breeze

4. Look! You don't have to take care of this now. Why don't you_____
   _____and we can talk about it some other time.
   a. shoot the breeze
   b. bite the dust
   c. put it on ice

5. It's no wonder nobody invites you to dinner. With your horrid table manners, you_____
   _____.
   a. turn everyone off
   b. like to hit the hay
   c. always hit the ceiling

6. Why don't you_____! Everyone is sick and tired of listening
   to you complain about how tough things are.
   a. go kick the bucket
   b. go fly a kite
   c. go hit the ceiling

7. Did you hear the news? Gary's rich aunt_____
   and left him a fortune!
   a. bit the dust
   b. hit the hay
   c. kicked the bucket

8. After we_____about the broken pipes in the bathroom,
   the building manager finally had them repaired.
   a. hit the ceiling
   b. raised a stink
   c. scratched his back

9. Unfortunately they lost, but they weren't the only ones who_____

    _____. Many other teams were also eliminated in the first round.
    a. jumped the gun
    b. bit the dust
    c. bent over backwards

10. Well, tomorrow's the big day! You'd better_____right now
    if you expect to play your best!
    a. go fly a kite
    b. bite the dust
    c. hit the hay

11. Don't go_____. There'll be plenty of time
    to tell them later. Why have them worry needlessly?
    a. jumping the gun
    b. raising a stink right now
    c. shooting the breeze with them

12. If a difficult situation comes up, a person shouldn't_____

    _____right away. He should attempt to control his anger until both sides of
    the question have been explored.
    a. turn someone off
    b. hit the ceiling
    c. raise a stink

13. When the need arose, Jud gave Trudy and Mitch his total support. He had never forgotten how

    they helped him find and move into his apartment. Now he felt that it was his turn to_____

    _____.
    a. bend over backwards for them
    b. scratch their backs
    c. cough up some much-needed cash

14. If you don't_____right now,
    I'll never lend you another thing as long as I live!
    a. fork over my necklace
    b. scratch my back
    c. shoot the breeze

II. Complete the sentences with idioms from the list below. Make any necessary changes in grammar and wording.

on ice	shoot the breeze
bite the dust	bend over backwards
hit the hay	cough up
jump the gun	scratch someone's back
hit the ceiling	fork over
turn someone off	go fly a kite
kick the bucket	raise a stink

1. The professor_____when he learned

   (became violently angry)

   that a copy of his final exam had disappeared from his desk drawer.

2. After the show they all went to a pizza parlor and sat around_____

   _____.

   (chatting informally)

3. It was only natural that we would_____.

   (protest strongly)

   After all, we stayed home all day waiting for the delivery truck and it never did show up.

4. If you can't come up with any new suggestions at this time, why don't you_____

   _____for now, and we'll get back to it tomorrow.

   (set the proposal aside for future use)

5. Your team needs more practice in passing the ball. Without a good workout, there's no doubt

   that you will_____and fail to make it to the finals.

   (be defeated)

6. Listen, my friend! If you keep abusing your body that way, you'll_____

   _____sooner than you expect!

   (die)

   You can't keep staying up night after night without any nourishment and expect not to suffer

   the consequences.

7. You're wondering why Caroline won't go out with you any more? Take a look at your clothes.

   You keep_____with the sloppy way you dress.

(disgusting her)

8. You expect me to be nice to them after the way they treated us the last time we were together?

   _____! I never want to talk to them again!

(go away)

9. Clearly they_____

(did something in haste)

   when they started to pack a week before their trip. There was no need to start so soon. After

   all, they were only going away for the weekend.

10. Since you're going to be up very late tomorrow night for New Year's Eve, I suggest that you

    _____tonight as soon as possible.

(go to bed)

    You won't want to get sleepy right in the middle of the festivities.

11. It's a shame that no one ever thinks of doing something nice for Jane. She's always

    _____for everybody and no one

(trying very hard to help someone out)

    seems to reciprocate.

12. After a great deal of "friendly persuasion," the boys finally_____

(handed over, gave unwillingly)

    _____the tennis shoes they had taken from Scott's locker.

13. If you teach me how to improve my tennis serve, I'll show you how to do those math

    problems that have been giving you so much trouble. What do you say? I'll_____

(return a favor)

    _____if you_____mine.

(return)

14. If you_____my basketball, I won't tell your folks that I saw you

(hand over, give)

    out with those guys who are always getting in trouble.

III. Complete the crossword puzzle using the clues below.

Across
3. set aside for future use
6. die
8. go down in defeat
10. disgust someone
11. hand over, give
13. chat informally
14. become very angry

Down
1. try very hard
2. go to bed
4. return a favor
5. protest strongly
7. give unwillingly
9. go away!
12. be hasty

Answer Key

I.   1. a
   2. b
   3. c
   4. c
   5. a

   6. b
   7. c
   8. a or b
   9. b
  10. c

  11. a or b
  12. b or c
  13. a or b
  14. a

II.   1. hit the ceiling
   2. shooting the breeze
   3. raise a stink
   4. put the proposal on ice
   5. bite the dust
   6. kick the bucket
   7. turning her off

   8. Go fly a kite
   9. jumped the gun
  10. hit the hay
  11. bending over backwards
  12. coughed up (or forked over)
  13. scratch your back, scratch
  14. fork over

III.

Section Five

Clothes Make the Man (and Woman)

45. Wet Blanket

What's Going On?   Ask the class the following questions:

What is covering the man in the picture? Would you say that the man under the blanket is on a friendly basis with the other man and woman? Judging from the facial expressions of the other man and woman, describe their attitude toward the man with the blanket. Why do you think they don't want to have anything to do with him? Do you think it is because of his appearance or for other reasons?

The Ball's in Your Court   Ask the class the following questions:

Describe how a wet blanket feels. If a person were like a wet blanket, what type of person would he be? How would you react to such a person? Have you ever been bored at a party? If so, what caused you to be bored? If you were out with a person who refused to share in the enthusiasm of the occasion, how would his attitude affect you? How do you think people would react to you if you acted bored in their presence?

It's Up to You   Present this situation to the students for discussion:

How would you describe a person who cast a shadow of gloom on a festive occasion by refusing to talk or interact with other people?

Play It by Ear   Have the students compose (orally or in writing) a skit based on the following situation:

John is ordinarily an outgoing person. Lately, he has had some personal problems and has become quite sullen. He was invited to a reception for a close colleague at work. Although he does not feel very festive, he decides to go because of loyalty to his friend. What will happen at the party?

46. Keep Under One's Hat

What's Going On?   Ask the class the following questions:

What does the man have under his hat? Why do you think he was covering it with his hat? What happened when the man removed his hat? Do you think the other man was curious about the object that was under the hat?

The Ball's in Your Court   Ask the class the following questions:

What are some ways in which people conceal things? Why might someone want to conceal something? Have you ever tried to keep something a secret? If so, under what circumstances? Have you ever revealed a secret? Can you think of any circumstances that would justify revealing a secret? How would you react if someone revealed information that you wanted kept secret? Do you see any similarity between *keeping something under one's hat* and *letting the cat out of the bag*? In what ways are these two expressions different?

It's Up to You   Present this situation to the students for discussion:

If you wanted somebody not to reveal a particular piece of information, what would you tell him to do?

Toot Your Own Horn   Have the students compose (orally or in writing) a dialogue based on the following situation:

Bob and Susan are students together at the university. They have many common interests and fall in love with each other. They decide to become engaged before graduating. Because they know their parents would not approve of their engagement at this time, they decide not to tell anyone of their decision until after graduation.

47. Up One's Sleeve

What's Going On?   Ask the class the following questions:

What is dropping out of the man's sleeve? Why do you think he had something up his sleeve in the first place? Do you think the man intended to drop what he had concealed? Do you think he has done something wrong? What makes you think so?

The Ball's in Your Court   Ask the class the following questions:

Why would anyone try to conceal something? Have you ever planned a surprise for someone and tried to conceal it? Why? Do you see any similarity between *keeping something under one's hat* and *having something up one's sleeve*? What do these two expressions have in common? How do they differ? Has anyone ever surprised you on a special occasion? If so, what was your reaction?

It's Up to You   Present this situation to the students for discussion:

Imagine that someone you know quite well is acting suspicious around you, as if he is hiding something from you. What might you wonder about him?

Play It by Ear   Have the students compose (orally or in writing) a skit or dialogue based on the following situation:

When Tony wakes up one morning his wife is especially nice to him. She cooks his favorite breakfast and brings him his robe and slippers. Tony can't quite understand why she is being so attentive today. He suspects that she must want something, but really has no idea what it could be. Later in the morning, Tony's wife tells him that she wants to go shopping.

48. Dressed to Kill

What's Going On?   Ask the class the following questions:

Describe the outfits the men are wearing. What is the man with the shield holding in his right hand? What is this instrument used for? How is the other man dressed? Why do you think the two men are dressed like this? What are they ready to do? What do the two men have in common?

The Ball's in Your Court   Ask the class the following questions:

How do you dress for different occasions? Do you wear your finest dress clothes to an informal gathering? Why not? Describe the types of clothes men and women wear to formal events. If you wanted to make a strong, positive impression on your host for a special event, what type of clothing would you wear? Do you think it would be better to be overdressed or underdressed for a particular occasion?

It's Up to You   Present this situation to the students for discussion:

What would you say about a woman who put on her finest, most elegant clothes to attend the opening night of the opera?

Toot Your Own Horn   Have the students compose (orally or in writing) a skit or dialogue based on the following situation:

Janet and Frances are guests at a formal ball in honor of a political candidate in one of the finest hotels of the city. Many professional and famous people are in attendance. Everyone is talking about the merits of the candidate. Janet and Frances are more interested in discussing how the women are dressed.

49. Give Someone the Slip

What's Going On?   Ask the class the following questions:

What do you suppose the police officer is thinking? What is he holding? How do you think he got it? Who got away? Did the person who got away leave quickly or slowly? Why?

The Ball's in Your Court   Ask the class the following questions:

Name some of the responsibilities of a police officer. How might a police officer try to stop someone who is trying to escape? If one person wanted to get away from another, would he most likely try to do so in a crowd or on an uncrowded street? Explain your answer. When a person "slips away" or "slips from someone's fingers," what has that person managed to do? Have you ever had the occasion to chase after someone? If so, were you able to catch this person or did he get away from you?

It's Up to You   Present this situation to the students for discussion:

Imagine that a robber successfully eluded the police after a robbery. How could you express the fact that the police were not able to catch him?

Play It by Ear   Have the students compose (orally or in writing) a skit based on the following situation:

Alberto and Carmen have been seeing each other for the past year. Carmen comes from a very traditional home and is not allowed to go out with a boy without a chaperone. Although a chaperone accompanies them on their outings, at times Alberto and Carmen do try to elude her so that they can be alone.

50. Knock Someone's Socks Off

What's Going On?   Ask the class the following questions:

What is in the pair of shoes? What is not in the shoes? What did the person do? Why do you think he did it? What do you think would cause a person to literally jump out of his socks? How do you think this person feels?

The Ball's in Your Court   Ask the class the following questions:

Have you ever been extremely excited about something? What do you feel like doing when you get excited? Describe several different situations that might enthuse people? How might people react to these situations? Do you think it would be easy or difficult to knock someone's socks off? Explain your answer.

It's Up to You   Present this situation to the students for discussion:

Imagine that you are a famous rock singer and you are performing privately for a group of teenagers in their home. What effect would your performance have on them?

Toot Your Own Horn   Have the students compose (orally or in writing) a skit or dialogue based on the following situation:

Several stereo enthusiasts are discussing the latest stereo equipment that's out on the market. They talk about compact disc players and the pure, full range of sound of the newest speakers. One member of the group is particularly enthused about his equipment and excitedly tells the others about its merits.

51. Talk Through One's Hat

What's Going On?   Ask the class the following questions:

What does the man with the hat appear to be doing? How is the other man responding? How would you characterize the statements of the man with the hat? What would you say about him, judging from his eyes? Does it appear that the man who is listening believes what he hears? Why do you think so?

The Ball's in Your Court   Ask the class the following questions:

Name some objects that can be used to amplify the voice. Do you think it is foolish to try to talk through a hat? What do you think the result would be? What would you think about a person who tried to do such a thing? Have you ever made any foolish statements? If so, describe the occasion. Has anyone ever said anything foolish to you? If so, what opinion did you form about that person?

It's Up to You   Present this situation to the students for discussion:

It is a known fact that smoking is bad for your health. If someone tried to tell you that smoking had no adverse effects on your health, what would you say about that person?

Toot Your Own Horn   Have the students compose (orally or in writing) a skit or dialogue based on the following situation:

A group of people are gathered around a modern painting in an art gallery. One of the spectators is animatedly discussing the painting with a great air of authority. A lot of the people seem interested in her observations. When she finishes, two art connoisseurs who were listening shake their heads in dismay.

52. Lose One's Shirt

What's Going On?   Ask the class the following questions:

What has happened to the man? How does he seem to feel? What is the horse wearing? Describe the attitude of the horse. What gives you this impression about the horse? What do you suppose the man is thinking about the horse? What might the horse be thinking about the man?

The Ball's in Your Court   Ask the class the following questions:

What are the possible outcomes of gambling? Name some different gambling activities. How do you suppose a person would feel if he lost a great deal of money? When a person gambles, is it possible to lose everything, including the clothing on one's back? Have you ever gambled? If so, have you lost or won? If you won, were you able to hold on to your winnings? Explain. Do you think that losing money can stop a person from gambling in the future?

It's Up to You Present this situation to the students for discussion:

What could you say to a person who tells you that she can win a great deal of money by gambling or betting?

Play It by Ear Have the students compose (orally or in writing) a skit or dialogue based on the following situation:

Mr. Jones has been investing in the stock market for a number of years. So far he has done rather well. Many of his stocks have doubled in value. Then, quite unexpectedly, the market crashes. Mr. Jones suffers great losses.

53. In Stitches

What's Going On? Ask the class the following questions:

What are the two men doing? What do you suppose is making them laugh so hard? How are they joined? What are the men holding? Why? Can one man get away from the other? How do you think the two men got into this situation in the first place?

The Ball's in Your Court Ask the class the following questions:

What can happen to a person when he laughs very hard? People laugh at different things. Name some situations or events that might make people laugh. What makes you laugh? Do all people laugh at the same things? Do people laugh only at funny things? Explain. Has anyone ever made fun of you? If so, describe the occasion. Have you ever made fun of anybody? If so, what was the reason? Were you doing it to be malicious?

It's Up to You Present this situation to the students for discussion:

Imagine that you are watching a hilarious movie. The actors are so funny that you are doubling over with laughter. What effect do the actors have on the audience?

Play It by Ear Have the students compose (orally or in writing) a skit or dialogue based on the following situation:

The Punch Club is famous for its performances by promising, upcoming comedians. The other night you and a group of friends went to the club to hear some comedians perform. Some of the jokes were very funny. Everyone in the group had a marvelous time. On the way home, you all discussed your evening.

54. Dressed to the Teeth

What's Going On? Ask the class the following questions:

How would you describe the woman's clothing? Is the woman happy or sad? How can you tell? Why do you think she is dressed this way? Is she trying to impress someone?

The Ball's in Your Court Ask the class the following questions:

How does a person dress when he wants to make a good impression on someone? Have you ever attended an elegant affair? If so, describe what you wore. Do you see any relationship between the expressions *dressed to kill* and *dressed to the teeth*? Are these expressions essentially the same? In your opinion, could they be used in identical situations?

It's Up to You   Present this situation to the students for discussion:

How would you describe a man who was dressed in all his finery?

Play It by Ear   Have the students compose (orally or in writing) a skit or dialogue based on the following situation:

It is the opening night of the ballet. The women who are attending the ballet wish to show off their designer gowns and their custom-designed jewelry. Although many of the women are opera buffs, they seem to be more interested in the show in the lobby than they are in the show on the stage. Pamela and Mary Beth meet in the lobby and discuss the sights they see around them.

All's Well That Ends Well

I. Select the best phrase to complete each sentence. In some cases, more than one answer is possible.

1. I had no idea that Ron was such a comic. He had us in stitches all night long. He even_____
   _____, and she hardly ever even smiles.
   a. had Katrina laughing
   b. had Katrina crying
   c. had Katrina enthused and excited

2. "If you promise to keep it under your hat, I'll let you know what they're up to."
   "Sure,_____."
   a. I'll keep it hidden
   b. I won't tell anyone
   c. I won't make any foolish statements

3. Believe me, the musical will knock your socks off! You_____
   _____!
   a. will hate it
   b. will want to see it in bare feet
   c. will really love it

4. "They lost their shirts on that business venture they started last year."
   "Yeah, I heard that_____
   _____."
   a. they were quite successful
   b. the business failed
   c. they went bankrupt

5. If you weren't such a wet blanket, everyone would_____
   _____.
   a. think you were boring
   b. enjoy your company more
   c. not criticize your taste in clothing

6. I can tell by the way you've been behaving that you've got something up your sleeve. Frankly,
   I'm curious to know_____.
   a. what you are planning
   b. what you're keeping secret
   c. what's wrong with your shirt

7. People_____even though
   she was dressed to the teeth.
   a. did not think she looked very good
   b. did not pay much attention to her
   c. thought she looked very elegant

8. When he said that he had an interview with the president, we all knew that he was talking through his hat. This isn't the first time we've caught him_____
_____.
   a. trying to keep something a secret
   b. wearing his finest clothing for the occasion
   c. making foolish, inaccurate statements

9. The Taylors were_____.
   They were at an elaborate fund-raising dinner, and everybody was dressed to kill.
   a. making a getaway
   b. wearing very elegant clothing
   c. planning a murder

10. It's not hard to figure out how she could have given them the slip. She just_____
_____.
    a. disappeared into the crowd
    b. handed them the garment and left
    c. ran down the street in front of them

II. Complete the sentences in the following dialogues with idioms from the list below. Make changes in grammar and wording where needed.

wet blanket	keep under one's hat
up one's sleeve	dressed to kill
give someone the slip	knock someone's socks off
talk through one's hat	lose one's shirt
in stitches	dressed to the teeth

Dialogue 1

Sara: Did you see Pat last night?

Anne: I sure did! She_____because Jeffrey had
                (had on her most elegant outfit)

asked her to go to the school dance with him.

Sara: But why would she want to go with him in the first place? He's such

_____!
      (a person who spoils the happiness of others)

Anne: You're right, but you know what they say: "Love is blind." Ever since I can remember,

he's always_____.
           (excited and enthused her)

Sara: Nevertheless, I'll bet that one of these days she'll realize what a loser he is and she'll

_____when he least expects it.
      (get away from him)

Anne: Well, we'll see about that!

Dialogue 2

Bob: OK, I'll tell you what's going on. But you've got to promise me you'll

_____.
           (keep it a secret)

Larry: You can count on me. My mouth is sealed. What's it all about?

Bob: Well, I'm sure you've noticed how funny George has been acting lately.

Larry: Yeah. I was wondering what_____.
           (he was hiding)

Bob: Well, he got in a card game the other night with some professional gamblers and he

_____.

(lost a great deal of money)

Larry: I see. I guess he doesn't know how to tell his wife, right?

Bob: That's right.

Dialogue 3

Al: Have you heard the latest news about Jane?

Gino: No. What's up?

Al: Bill told me that she_____

(had put on her most elaborate clothes)

in those gaudy clothes she uses in her comic act and that she had her audience

_____.

(laughing so hard they were holding their sides)

Gino: Is he talking about the Jane we know, or is this someone he's imagining?

Al: We both know that Bill has a tendency to_____

(make foolish, inaccurate statements)

_____, but I think he's right on this one. He was in the audience

himself. He spoke with her after the show, and she told him she was even offered

a six-week contract.

Gino: Wow! I'm amazed!

III. Unscramble the following idioms. (The apostrophes are placed in their correct positions in the words.)

1. tew kbtlena
   _____

2. epke dunre eso'n ath
   _____

3. pu ens'o evlees
   _____

4. sdreeds ot lilk
   _____

5. vige mneeoso het pils
   _____

6. conkk nsomoes'e okscs fof
   _____

7. kalt rothugh nos'e tha
   _____

8. sloe nos'e thris
   _____

9. ni chitstes
   _____

10. serdeds ot hte ethet
    _____

Answer Key

I. 1. a   5. b   9. b
    2. b   6. a or b   10. a
    3. c   7. a or b
    4. b or c   8. c

II. **Dialogue 1**

was dressed to kill (or was dressed to the teeth), a wet blanket, knocked her socks off, give him the slip

Dialogue 2

keep it under your hat, he had up his sleeve, lost his shirt

Dialogue 3

was dressed to the teeth (or was dressed to kill), in stitches, talk through his hat

III. 1. wet blanket   6. knock someone's socks off
     2. keep under one's hat   7. talk through one's hat
     3. up one's sleeve   8. lose one's shirt
     4. dressed to kill   9. in stitches
     5. give someone the slip   10. dressed to the teeth

Section Six

When Things Go Wrong

55. Lemon

What's Going On?   Ask the class the following questions:

What is the man riding in? How would you say he feels? What makes you think so? Does he appear to be getting a smooth ride? Does the vehicle seem to be in good condition? What kind of fruit does the vehicle resemble?

The Ball's in Your Court   Ask the class the following questions:

What does a lemon taste like? Which would taste better to you, something sweet or something bitter? Would you avoid tasting something that you did not like? Name some other fruits and describe how they taste. Have you ever purchased something that was defective? What did you do about it? Describe some ways in which things can be defective.

It's Up to You   Present this situation to the students for discussion:

Mrs. Nogara purchased a washing machine, but unfortunately she had trouble with it from the very beginning. It required constant repairs. How would you describe the machine?

Play It by Ear   Have the students compose (orally or in writing) a skit or dialogue based on the following situation:

One day Mr. Jordan bought a new toaster as a surprise for his wife, since their old toaster was broken. The next morning, the Jordans are excited about having some toast for breakfast, but their enthusiasm turns to disappointment when the toaster fails to work properly and burns the toast. Of course the Jordans are very upset. They decide to take the toaster back to the store where they got it.

56. Out of the Woods

What's Going On?   Ask the class the following questions:

Where is the man? What is surrounding the bed? Who is peering out from behind a tree? What does the man's expression tell you? Do you think the man is safe? Explain your answer.

The Ball's in Your Court   Ask the class the following questions:

What are some of the dangers of being in the woods? Name some animals that are found in the woods. Are all these animals dangerous? Have you ever been in a dangerous position? If so, describe it. What can a person do to protect himself from danger in a forest? How would you feel if you were successful in avoiding or getting out of some danger?

It's Up to You   Present this situation to the students for discussion:

Imagine that a friend of yours is trying to get out of a difficult financial situation but has not yet been able to do so. What could you say about him?

Toot Your Own Horn   Have the students compose (orally or in writing) a dialogue or skit based on the following situation:

Jim and Oscar are talking about their final examinations. Oscar is particularly worried since his grades were rather low last year. He was in danger of being dismissed from the college if his grades did not improve. He made a conscientious effort to improve, and his grades picked up. However, he must do well on his final exams in order to keep improving his grade point average, since he is still on probation. He's not yet out of danger.

57. Get Up on the Wrong Side of the Bed

What's Going On?   Ask the class the following questions:

Where is the bed? Why do you think the woman looks confused? Why is the blanket hanging over the edge of the bed? What do you think happened to the other person who was in the bed? Do you think he was fully awake when he tried to get out of bed?

The Ball's in Your Court   Ask the class the following questions:

How do people usually feel when they have to get out of bed after having had very little sleep? Have you ever been in a bad mood? How did you get in that mood? What did you do to work your way out of it? How did you behave toward other people when you were feeling crabby? Describe some situations that might put people in a bad mood. How do other people usually react to a person who is feeling out of sorts?

It's Up to You   Present this situation to the students for discussion:

Imagine that your teacher entered the classroom without her usual warm greeting and immediately proceeded to hand out a surprise examination in spite of the protests of the students. What would you say about your teacher's mood?

Toot Your Own Horn   Have the students compose (orally or in writing) a skit or dialogue based on the following situation:

Mary and Anna work as tellers at a bank. They are talking about Mrs. Payne, their supervisor. When she came to work this morning, she began to complain about the inaccuracy of the records turned in the day before and about the rudeness of the tellers with their customers. Of course, Mary and Anna feel that Mrs. Payne's complaints are totally unjustified. Usually Mrs. Payne is much more cheery and does not reproach the employees in this manner.

58. Out on a Limb

What's Going On?   Ask the class the following questions:

What is the man hanging from? Does the branch seem sturdy? What is the man trying to do? What could happen to the man? How did he get himself into this position? Do you think the cat looks worried? In your opinion, would the man or the cat be more likely to land safely on the ground if the branch broke? Why?

The Ball's in Your Court   Ask the class the following questions:

Have you ever been in a precarious situation? If so, how did you get into it? What did you do to get out of it? Did anyone help you? Have you ever offered to do a favor for someone who needed your help? If so, what were the circumstances? Would you take a risk to help a friend who was unreliable? Why or why not? Under what circumstances would you risk your reputation by allowing your name to be used as a reference for a friend?

It's Up to You   Present this situation to the students for discussion:

If an unreliable friend asked you to lend him some money and you agreed to do so, what would you be doing?

Play It by Ear   Have the students compose (orally or in writing) a skit or dialogue based on the following situation:

Eric's cousin Stan wants to buy a car; however, Stan has not had a steady income for the past year. He asks Eric to guarantee his loan with the bank. Eric is hesitant to sign the papers. He does not want to be responsible for the payments if his cousin defaults. Nevertheless, because Stan is his cousin, Eric agrees to sign the papers.

59. Eating Someone

What's Going On?   Ask the class the following questions:

What kind of animals are shown in the picture? What are they doing? How do snakes usually eat their prey? Do you think certain types of snakes are capable of swallowing other, smaller snakes? What do snakes usually eat? Describe the attitudes of the snakes in the picture. What do their eyes tell you?

The Ball's in Your Court   Ask the class the following questions:

Describe some different types of snakes and tell where they are found. What other animals or insects are often annoying to human beings? Why are they annoying? What do they do? Do some of them bite? What are the effects of their bites? What should you do if you are bitten? Name some other sources of annoyance (besides animals). Describe an occasion when you have been upset. What or who upset you? What do you feel like when you are upset?

It's Up to You   Present this situation to the students for discussion:

Karen has been out of sorts all day long. She has consistently refused to explain why she is so irritable. If you wanted to know what was bothering her, what would you ask her?

Play It by Ear   Have the students compose (orally or in writing) a skit or dialogue based on the following situation:

You have grown up with Joanne and know when she is happy or sad. Lately you can tell that something is really bothering her, even though she will not admit it. You show your concern by telling her that you know something is upsetting her. You ask her to be honest with you and to share her concerns with you. After all, what are friends for?

60. Get the Ax

What's Going On?   Ask the class the following questions:

What has happened to the little man? How does he feel about what has happened to him? What is the tall man doing? What does he seem to be saying to the little man? What does the tall man's facial expression tell you about his attitude toward the little man? Do you think the tall man is enjoying what he is doing?

The Ball's in Your Court   Ask the class the following questions:

What is an ax ordinarily used for? Is the word *sever* related to one of the functions of an ax? What takes place when a person is fired or discharged from his job? Name some reasons why a person might be dismissed from his job. Are people always discharged because of faulty performance on the job? Have you ever had occasion to sever your relationship with a particular business enterprise? What made you do so?

It's Up to You Present this situation to the students for discussion:

Tom consistently arrives late for work and takes time off without calling or providing an explanation. Do you think he will be able to keep his job? What do you suppose might happen to him?

Toot Your Own Horn Have the students compose (orally or in writing) a skit or dialogue based on the following situation:

Gail has a summer job as a waitress in a restaurant. However, many of her friends are not working, and they often invite her to go shopping or spend a day at the beach with them. Because Gail wants to have fun with her friends, she often calls in sick when she should be at work. One day Gail's boss goes to the shopping center during his lunch hour. He sees Gail there, shopping with some friends, even though she called that morning to say she was sick. What do you think will happen when Gail goes to work the next day?

61. In the Hole

What's Going On? Ask the class the following questions:

In what direction is the sign pointing? What is the sign pointing to? Where do the stairs lead? Does it appear to be an inviting place? How would you describe it? Why do you suppose this business establishment is in a hole? Do you think Peter's Hardware Store was originally built above the ground?

The Ball's in Your Court Ask the class the following questions:

Do you know of any stores that are located in a basement? If so, are they as popular as the taller, more outstanding department stores? How would you feel if you were sitting or standing in a hole? When a person does not have enough money to meet his financial obligations, how does he feel? If a person is in debt, what must he do to get out of debt? Name some ways in which people get into debt.

It's Up to You Present this situation to the students for discussion:

If you wanted to purchase a home and had to borrow money from a bank in order to do so, what would you be doing?

Play It by Ear Have the students compose (orally or in writing) a skit or dialogue based on the following situation:

Mr. Montesinos wants to build an addition onto his home; however, he does not have enough money to pay for the construction. He decides to pay a visit to his banker friend, Mr. Murdock, and ask him for a loan. Mr. Montesinos realizes that he will end up owing the bank a great deal of money, but since he has no other big outstanding financial obligations, he feels certain that he will be able to handle the monthly payments for the next several years. Describe the conversation between the two men.

62. Bite the Bullet

What's Going On? Ask the class the following questions:

What has happened to the man? Where did the bullet land? What is the man doing to the bullet? Is this an easy thing to do? How do you think the man feels about the situation he's in? Has he survived the initial blow?

The Ball's in Your Court   Ask the class the following questions:

If a person were in pain, what might make it easier to endure the pain? Do you think that biting on something would help? What are other ways to alleviate pain? Have you ever undergone a great upset? What did you do to feel better? What qualities do you think a person should possess in order to endure in a difficult situation?

It's Up to You   Present this situation to the students for discussion:

Imagine that you were trapped on the roof of a burning building, waiting for a safety net to arrive so you could jump to safety. What would you have to do until help arrived?

Play It by Ear   Have the students compose (orally or in writing) a skit or dialogue based on the following situation:

Nancy and Jim, who are newlyweds, generally spend most of their free time together. However, one day Jim decided to go out after work with some of his friends from the office. He failed to call his wife, who had hurried home from work and was busily preparing his favorite dinner. Nancy was looking forward to spending a quiet, intimate evening at home with Jim. When Jim got ready to leave the restaurant with his friends, he suddenly remembered he had forgotten to tell Nancy his plans. He knew she would be worried and angry with him. Jim was reluctant to face his wife's anger and disappointment, but he hurried home to apologize to her. When Jim walked in the door, Nancy let him know how she felt in no uncertain terms! Jim endured her wrath quietly. The next day at the office, one of Jim's friends asks him what happened when he got home the night before.

63. Face the Music

What's Going On?   Ask the class the following questions:

What instrument is the musician playing? What are the large objects on either side of the musician? What purpose do they serve? What type of clothing is the shorter man wearing? Judging from his uniform, in what type of institution do you think he lives? Do you think he likes the music? How can you tell? What must he endure? Would you say that having to endure something unpleasant can be a type of punishment?

The Ball's in Your Court   Ask the class the following questions:

If a person does something wrong, what must he be prepared to do? Do you think that people eventually have to pay for their wrongdoing? Explain your answer. Explain the meaning of the saying "you reap what you sow." Can a person be rewarded as well as punished for his actions? Have you ever done something against someone else's wishes? What was the outcome? Have you ever reprimanded someone? If so, for what reason? In your opinion, is corporal punishment justified? If so, under what circumstances? Which do you think is worse, physical punishment or mental punishment?

It's Up to You   Present this situation to the students for discussion:

The police apprehended a gang of hoodlums who were defacing public property. Now that the members of the gang have been caught, what will happen to them?

Play It by Ear   Have the students compose (orally or in writing) a skit or dialogue based on the following situation:

Phillip is sixteen years old and has just recently gotten his driver's license. His father lets him use the family car for certain, special occasions; however, he insists on knowing who Phillip is with and where he is going. Today Phillip wanted to drive to the beach with some friends. He tried getting in touch with his dad at work, but he was out of the office. Phillip decided to take the car without his father's permission. In doing so, he knew full well that his father would be angry with him. What do you think will happen to Phillip?

64. Blow It

What's Going On?   Ask the class the following questions:

What occasion are the man and woman celebrating? What did the woman do? What happened to the man? How do you think he feels? How would you say the woman feels? Do you think the woman intended to do what she did? What was the woman trying to do? Was she successful?

The Ball's in Your Court   Ask the class the following questions:

What other occasions call for a celebration? In what ways can people celebrate? Have you ever failed to accomplish something even though you tried very hard to succeed? If so, describe the situation. Did you blame yourself for the failure? How did you feel? Was the failure an embarrassment to you? Did your lack of success affect anyone but you? Were others concerned about what happened to you?

It's Up to You   Present this situation to the students for discussion:

The score is tied. Ariel's basketball team has a chance to win the game if she can make the winning point with a free throw. Unfortunately, she misses the shot. What would you say about Ariel?

Play It by Ear   Have the students compose (orally or in writing) a skit or dialogue based on the following situation:

Ted has been working for a commercial art firm for two years. He has been doing excellent work, and the head of the firm has promised him a promotion and a raise in salary if he can convince the XYZ Corporation to let his company handle all of its commercial advertising. Because of an unexpected emergency, Ted fails to show up for the meeting with the executives of XYZ Corporation and consequently loses the account for his firm. What will the head of Ted's firm say to him?

65. At the End of One's Rope

What's Going On?   Ask the class the following questions:

What is the man hanging on to? How would you describe the position he's in? Judging from his facial expression, how do you think he feels? Why? How much longer do you think he can hang on? What will happen if he lets go of the rope? What kind of animal is beneath him? How would you describe it? Is this type of animal dangerous? Why? What is its natural habitat?

The Ball's in Your Court   Ask the class the following questions:

Name several different occasions that might cause stress in a person. What can happen to a person who is under stress? How might he feel? Can a person keep on reacting in a positive manner when he is feeling pressured? What can a person do to cope with a situation that is difficult, if not impossible, to handle? What type of personality does a person need to have in order to cope with an adverse situation? What could happen to a person when he reaches the limit of his ability to persevere in an intolerable situation?

It's Up to You   Present this situation to the students for discussion:

A friend of yours tells you that she just quit her job because she could no longer put up with the unjust treatment she was receiving from her supervisor. How might you explain her reason for leaving?

Toot Your Own Horn   Have the students compose (orally or in writing) a dialogue based on the following situation:

Mr. Robertson is directing a documentary film on the tribal customs of the natives of a recently discovered Polynesian island. From the very beginning, he has had problems that have caused delays in filming the picture. The natives of the island have been uncooperative, the weather has been bad, and many of the crew members have fallen ill. As a result, he's already over budget. Mr. Robertson is discussing his troubles with a close friend and asks his friend's advice. He feels that he can't keep putting up with all the setbacks and wonders if he should ask to be released from his obligation.

66. On One's Last Legs

What's Going On?   Ask the class the following questions:

On how many legs is the animal in the illustration standing? What is he playing? Do you think he will be able to maintain his position for much longer? What do you suppose happened to his other legs? What do you think will happen if the remaining leg is incapacitated?

The Ball's in Your Court   Ask the class the following questions:

What can happen when a person loses confidence in himself? Have you ever known anybody who was unable to carry on his work or obligations because of illness? If so, describe this person's former situation and compare it with his present one. What are some different ways in which a person can become incapacitated? When a person is destitute, how might he feel about his future?

It's Up to You   Present this situation to the students for discussion:

What would you say about a person who was sick, in debt, and had no prospects for a job?

Toot Your Own Horn   Have the students compose (orally or in writing) a skit or dialogue based on the following situation:

Gibson and Company was a big industrial firm. The company was founded by Mr. Gibson's grandfather and was very successful during the war years. However, after the war, when government contracts became fewer and fewer, the company went bankrupt. Although Mr. Gibson now has another job, he has never recovered physically or mentally from the blow of losing the company his grandfather founded. One day some of his coworkers are discussing how old and defeated he looks.

67. Hot Under the Collar

What's Going On? Ask the class the following questions:

What seems to be coming out from under the man's collar? What does his facial expression tell you about how he is feeling? Why do you suppose he feels that way? Does the man seem very likely to cool off? What effect does a collar have if it is too tight?

The Ball's in Your Court Ask the class the following questions:

When a person becomes angry, does he usually act excited or calm? What happens physically to a person when he becomes angry? Give some examples of situations that might make someone angry. What are some different ways that people react when they are angry? When a person is extremely angry, does real smoke come out from under his collar? How do you feel when you are very hot? Do you think that some people become angry more quickly than others? Do all people get angry at the same things? Does it take a lot to make you angry? Explain your answer. How do you react when something or someone makes you mad? What are some of your pet peeves?

It's Up to You Present this situation to the students for discussion:

Mrs. Rose asked her daughter Michelle to watch her little brother while she went out to do some errands. When Mrs. Rose came home and found that Michelle had gone out with a friend, how do you think she reacted?

Toot Your Own Horn Have the students compose (orally or in writing) a skit or dialogue based on the following situation:

You are out driving your brand new car. While you're stopped at a stoplight, someone drives into the back of your car and causes extensive damage to the rear bumper and trunk. The driver of the other car gets out and tells you that the light had turned green and that you should have started to move forward. He claims that the accident was not his fault and that you were responsible for it.

68. On the Line

What's Going On? Ask the class the following questions:

On what is the man balancing? Is he having a difficult time? Why is he waving his hands? Do you think he will lose his balance? What makes you think so? Where are tightrope walkers usually found?

The Ball's in Your Court Ask the class the following questions:

What kinds of skills are required to walk a tightrope? What feelings do you think tightrope walkers experience? What causes these feelings? When a person is walking a tightrope, do you think he has to concentrate more than usual? Why? What would happen if he were to take a false step? Do you think the feelings experienced by tightrope walkers are like those experienced by race car drivers and trapeze artists? Why or why not? What do these activities have in common? Would you say that swimmers or ball players experience identical feelings of anxiety? Why or why not? Have you ever been in danger of not succeeding in a particular undertaking if you made a single mistake? If so, how did you feel?

It's Up to You Present this situation to the students for discussion:

If there were some reason to believe that a person running for office had lied about his qualifications, what would you say about his reputation?

Play It by Ear   Have the students compose (orally or in writing) a dialogue or skit based on the following situation:

A famous pianist had always enjoyed the respect of the musical world. However, her last several concerts were considerably below her usual level of performance. Her upcoming concert at Carnegie Hall is of vital importance to her career, since many of New York's foremost music critics will be in attendance. She knows that she must play like she's never played before, or her career will suffer. On the morning of the concert, she discusses her concerns with a friend.

All's Well That Ends Well

I. Complete the sentences with idioms from the list below. Make changes in grammar and wording where needed.

lemon
get up on the wrong side of the bed
eating someone
in the hole
face the music
at the end of one's rope
hot under the collar

out of the woods
out on a limb
get the ax
bite the bullet
blow it
on one's last legs
on the line

1. I knew that the poor guy was_____, but I didn't know that he had actually been taken to the hospital! What are they treating him for?

2. It was obvious that something had been_____ all day long. She was uncommunicative and irritable with everybody. We just couldn't imagine what was upsetting her.

3. I don't think you should quit your job just because you're_____ _____. You're not the only one who got angry with the foreman. None of us liked the way we were being treated. Don't worry, it'll pass.

4. Although they have paid off most of their debts, they're still not_____ _____. Even with both of them working, they won't be able to pay off all their bills until sometime next year.

5. After the earthquake, many people who were trapped under the rubble of fallen buildings had to_____until rescue teams could dig them out.

6. Mr. Smithers simply could not adhere to company policy. He was quite outspoken about the inferior working conditions and lack of recreational facilities for the employees. It's no wonder that he finally_____.

7. When Joan walked in filled with complaints, we all guessed that she had_____ _____. Her mood was simply intolerable all day long.

8. You must realize that you're putting your reputation_____ by vouching for his honesty. He's got a history of lying, you know.

9. Very frankly, I'm_____. I can't deal with all this inefficiency any longer.

10. We must be careful. Since credit is so freely given these days, it would be easy to go_____ _____.

11. Bob knew that he would have to_____eventually. It's impossible for a person to maintain such a strenuous routine without suffering some ill effects.

12. Aaron knew that Michael wasn't right for the job and that he would be going_____ _____ by recommending him for the position. If Michael did not work out, he'd be held responsible.

13. Jim was convinced that he_____at the audition. You can imagine his surprise when the orchestra director offered him a two-year contract.

14. Mrs. Simpson suspected that she had gotten_____ from the moment she started using her new washing machine. Not only did it make funny noises, but it constantly overflowed as well.

II. Match the situation in column A with the idiom in column B.

A

_____ 1. He'll never learn! It doesn't pay to constantly put yourself out for your friends. Many times people tend to be unappreciative.

_____ 2. That player is really concentrating. Is this a crucial match?

_____ 3. Didn't I warn you not to buy that brand of TV set? I told you that you would have nothing but trouble with it.

_____ 4. Unfortunately, many people spend far more than they should. Credit cards can be a disadvantage as well as an advantage!

_____ 5. Did Herb finally pay off all his debts?

_____ 6. Why aren't you working today? Is this your day off?

_____ 7. Ordinarily she wouldn't go slamming around like that. What's gotten into her?

_____ 8. It's not surprising that no agreement was reached during the discussions. Everyone was so upset!

_____ 9. From the moment we walked in, we could sense that Jonathan was not himself. We knew he was worried about something, but he just wouldn't open up.

_____ 10. Don't worry! We'll soon know the test results. Just hold on a little while longer.

_____ 11. I can't understand why the motor keeps dying. I just had it repaired.

_____ 12. No one can figure out why Edgar has been so depressed and gloomy lately.

_____ 13. Jack's always complaining about the high cost of maintaining his car. It gets such poor gas mileage!

_____ 14. Sheila had to get away for several days because she felt so harassed by the pressures of family and work.

B

a. Yes, but the salesman said it was a reliable set. I didn't dream it would turn out to be such a lemon!

b. Almost. He's still not completely out of the woods.

c. I, for one, avoid going out on a limb for anyone. Whenever I do, I end up getting hurt one way or another.

d. Well, his title's on the line.

e. Do you know what could be eating him?

f. Yeah. He should perk up. He's acting like he's on his last legs.

g. Actually, I got the ax for misplacing a bunch of accounts. The company lost a lot of money because they weren't mailed out.

h. That's for sure! And once you're in the hole, it's not very easy to get out.

i. Well, it's hard to be reasonable when someone gets so hot under the collar.

j. Don't ask me! She must have gotten up on the wrong side of the bed. She's been like that all day.

k. True, but everyone warned him about that before he bought it. Now he's got to face the music.

l. I don't blame her. She was really at the end of her rope!

m. I'm sick and tired of biting the bullet! I've got to know if the operation is really necessary.

n. The guy who worked on it really blew it. You should have taken the car to someone more experienced.

III. Find and circle the following idioms. Be sure to look horizontally, vertically, and diagonally.

lemon
get up on the wrong side of the bed
eating someone
in the hole
face the music
at the end of one's rope
hot under the collar

out of the woods
out on a limb
get the ax
bite the bullet
blow it
on one's last legs
on the line

x	a	t	t	h	e	e	n	d	o	f	o	n	e	s	r	o	p	e	p	q	r	t	a	b	n	d	y
a	d	e	j	k	m	h	o	t	u	n	d	e	r	t	h	e	c	o	l	l	a	r	g	f	c	b	i
d	f	z	b	t	o	f	s	i	n	t	h	e	h	o	l	e	k	d	l	m	b	j	t	r	d	j	n
j	p	q	n	s	k	u	l	p	d	d	r	t	p	x	d	y	z	b	t	e	i	a	g	t	l	c	r
g	e	t	u	p	o	n	t	h	e	w	r	o	n	g	s	i	d	e	o	f	t	h	e	b	e	d	l
r	v	w	b	h	i	e	v	o	r	f	p	q	s	t	h	e	p	l	u	l	e	f	t	p	m	k	p
p	u	m	l	c	d	g	h	l	f	v	n	c	p	t	r	q	n	s	t	d	t	g	t	d	o	q	m
t	n	v	o	u	y	x	p	o	n	t	h	e	l	i	n	e	d	d	o	u	h	s	h	m	n	r	x
s	d	v	w	o	p	h	r	s	d	f	h	g	t	r	s	y	w	f	n	d	e	r	e	f	g	d	s
e	a	t	i	n	g	s	o	m	e	o	n	e	f	c	k	t	m	o	a	v	b	l	a	b	t	r	n
y	w	x	t	e	d	j	d	o	j	k	b	r	w	d	b	n	j	s	l	e	u	m	x	y	l	b	k
x	h	y	k	d	t	y	n	l	r	q	p	c	f	o	m	p	l	n	i	h	l	r	b	d	r	t	l
k	q	f	a	c	e	t	h	e	m	u	s	i	c	x	o	f	c	g	m	d	l	s	f	k	g	d	e
j	p	z	o	s	m	d	p	b	r	w	q	n	d	h	c	d	h	i	b	n	e	p	j	n	t	l	r
d	l	j	d	n	r	s	a	u	k	d	u	o	n	o	n	e	s	l	a	s	t	l	e	g	s	p	b

Answer Key

I.   1. on his last legs
     2. eating her
     3. hot under the collar
     4. out of the woods
     5. bite the bullet
     6. got the ax
     7. gotten up on the wrong side of the bed

     8. on the line
     9. at the end of my rope
     10. in the hole
     11. face the music
     12. out on a limb
     13. blew it
     14. a lemon

II. 1. c
     2. d
     3. a
     4. h
     5. b

     6. g
     7. j
     8. i
     9. e
     10. m

     11. n
     12. e or f
     13. k
     14. l

III.

```
x  a  t  t  h  e  e  n  d  o  f  o  n  e  s  r  o  p  e  p  q  r  t  a  b  n  d  y
a  d  e  j  k  m  h  o  t  u  n  d  e  r  t  h  e  c  o  l  l  a  r  g  f  c  b  i
d  f  z  b  t  o  f  s  i  n  t  h  e  h  o  l  e  k  d  l  m  b  j  t  r  d  j  n
j  p  q  n  s  k  u  l  p  d  d  r  t  p  x  d  y  z  b  t  e  i  a  g  t  l  c  r
g  e  t  u  p  o  n  t  h  e  w  r  o  n  g  s  i  d  e  o  f  t  h  e  b  e  d  l
r  v  w  b  h  i  e  v  o  r  f  p  q  s  t  h  e  p  l  u  l  e  f  t  p  m  k  p
p  u  m  l  c  d  g  h  l  f  v  n  c  p  t  r  q  n  s  t  d  t  g  t  d  o  q  m
t  n  v  o  u  y  x  p  o  n  t  h  e  l  i  n  e  d  d  o  u  h  s  h  m  n  r  x
s  d  v  w  o  p  h  r  s  d  f  h  g  t  r  s  y  w  f  n  d  e  r  e  f  g  d  s
e  a  t  i  n  g  s  o  m  e  o  n  e  f  c  k  t  m  o  a  v  b  l  a  b  t  r  n
y  w  x  t  e  d  j  d  o  j  k  b  r  w  d  b  n  j  s  l  e  u  m  x  y  l  b  k
x  h  y  k  d  t  y  n  l  r  q  p  c  f  o  m  p  l  n  i  h  l  r  b  d  r  t  l
k  q  f  a  c  e  t  h  e  m  u  s  i  c  x  o  f  c  g  m  d  l  s  f  k  g  d  e
j  p  z  o  s  m  d  p  b  r  w  q  n  d  h  c  d  h  i  b  n  e  p  j  n  t  l  r
d  l  j  d  n  r  s  a  u  k  d  u  o  n  o  n  e  s  l  a  s  t  l  e  g  s  p  b
```

Section Seven

When Things Go Well

69. For a Song

What's Going On?   Ask the class the following questions:

What musical instrument do you think the man is playing? Does he seem to enjoy what he is doing? How can you tell? How are other people reacting to his performance? What are they throwing at the man? Do you think they like what they hear? Do you think the man expected to get paid for his singing? Why or why not? Why do you suppose the man keeps singing in spite of the unfavorable reaction of his audience?

The Ball's in Your Court   Ask the class the following questions:

People have different reasons for learning to play a musical instrument. What are some of them? Do musicians usually get paid a lot of money for performing? Name some situations in which they do and some in which they don't. Do you think that most people who write songs are able to sell them for a lot of money? Do you think that most songs that are written are published and recorded? Explain your answer. How would you measure the value of a song? Have you ever purchased an expensive item for a very low price? If so, were you satisfied with your purchase?

It's Up to You   Present this situation to the students for discussion:

A friend of yours tells you that she was able to pick up a valuable piece of furniture for next to nothing. What would you say?

Play It by Ear   Have the students compose (orally or in writing) a skit or dialogue based on the following situation:

While shopping one day, you saw a beautiful coat that you wanted to buy. Unfortunately, it was priced very high and you were unable to purchase it. At a later date, while browsing in the store, you notice that the coat is on sale. The coat is not only on sale, but there is an additional 20% off the sale price. You decide to buy the coat, and when you take it to the cashier he informs you—much to your delight—that an additional 25% will be taken off at the cash register. On your way home, you run into a friend and tell her about your good fortune.

70. Make a Splash

What's Going On?   Ask the class the following questions:

What is the man falling into? What is he smoking? How do you think he is feeling? How can you tell? Would you say that the man is successful? What do you think people would say if they saw a man falling into a pile of money?

The Ball's in Your Court   Ask the class the following questions:

What happens when a person falls or jumps into a swimming pool? When people are playing and splashing in a pool, do they attract attention? How? Why? Have you ever been the center of attention? If so, describe the situation. What must a person do to keep attention focused on him? In your opinion, do successful people always draw attention, or are they sometimes inconspicuous? Give some examples to support your opinion.

It's Up to You   Present this situation to the students for discussion:

A new rock group has just released an album and is starting a concert tour. Every night their concerts are sold out, and every day they receive excellent reviews. What would you say about the impact this group is having on the public?

Toot Your Own Horn Have the students compose (orally or in writing) a dialogue based on the following situation:

Carol and Virginia are discussing the latest mystery novel by Jonathan Keeton. This is his fifth novel. It hit the bookstores scarcely a month ago, and already it is number three on the best-seller list. There is no doubt that this novel will continue to draw just as much attention as the other four did, not only in this country, but also abroad.

71. Have the World by the Tail

What's Going On? Ask the class the following questions:

Where is the man? What is he wearing? How would you guess he is feeling? Why? What is he holding? To what is it attached? What do you suppose the man is doing out in space? Would you say that he is in control of the world, or that the world is in control of him?

The Ball's in Your Court Ask the class the following questions:

What are some of the resources that the world has to offer? In what ways do they benefit people? If a person had all the resources of the world at his disposal, how do you think he would feel? Why? Have you ever been in a situation where everything has worked out very well and smoothly for you? If so, describe it and tell how you felt.

It's Up to You Present this situation to the students for discussion:

What would you say about a person who had no cares or worries and was totally happy with his life?

Play It by Ear Have the students compose (orally or in writing) a skit or dialogue based on the following situation:

Judith, who is a busy and respected physician, has just announced her engagement to Rodney, a very successful corporate lawyer. They want to marry soon, and are busy making preparations for the wedding. They plan to go on an extended trip to Europe for their honeymoon. When they return, their new home will be waiting for them. At this point in their lives, Judith and Rodney don't have a care in the world. At an engagement party, Judith and Rodney describe their situation to friends and relatives.

72. Sitting Pretty

What's Going On? Ask the class the following questions:

Who are the people in the illustration? What are they wearing? What are they sitting on? What are they holding? How do you think they are feeling? What makes you think so? Do you think they are comfortable? In what ways are they comfortable?

The Ball's in Your Court Ask the class the following questions:

Have you ever been in a position where you felt extremely fortunate? If so, describe it. How would you define *fortunate*? Name some things that make people feel fortunate. Do you think money can bring people happiness? Why or why not? Do you think it is possible for people to be happy even if they are poor? Explain your answer. What would you do if you won a large sum of money? Do you think it would help you become a better person? Would it make you any happier? Do you think that money corrupts people? Explain your answers.

It's Up to You Present this situation to the students for discussion:

How would you describe a person who had plenty of money, a beautiful wardrobe, an expensive car, and a large, beautiful home?

Toot Your Own Horn Have the students compose (orally or in writing) a dialogue or skit based on the following situation:

While rummaging through her attic the other day, Lori happened to run across a box full of old letters from overseas that her grandfather had been saving. The letters had some interesting-looking stamps, so she took them to a dealer to be appraised. Much to her surprise, the stamps turned out to be worth a great deal of money. She sold them, and now finds that she can lead the type of life that she has always dreamed of. Lori is discussing her good fortune with her friend Doris over lunch one day.

73. Feel Like a Million Dollars

What's Going On? Ask the class the following questions:

What is the man holding? Why do you think he is positioning his own face on the bill? Comment on the man's general appearance and on his state of mind. Why do you think he feels so happy? Do you know if there is such a thing as a million-dollar bill? If there was, where might it be used?

The Ball's in Your Court Ask the class the following questions:

Can you think of a particular event in your life that made you feel wonderful? Name some different things that might make people feel good. Is money the only thing that can make a person feel good? What do you think a million dollars would feel like? Have you ever felt like a million dollars? Do you see any relationship between *having the world by the tail* and *feeling like a million dollars?* How are these expressions similar? How do they differ? How would you feel if you had a million dollars? Do you think people would treat you differently if you were wealthy? Why or why not?

It's Up to You Present this situation to the students for discussion:

What might you say about yourself if you had recovered from a lengthy illness and were now feeling strong, vigorous, and in the best of health?

Toot Your Own Horn Have the students compose (orally or in writing) a skit or dialogue based on the following situation:

Lately you have been working very hard. Your friends tell you that you'd better start to take it easy, or else you will become ill. On their advice, you make plans to spend some time at a resort. There you relax completely. You play tennis, go swimming, and lie in the sun. When you return, people comment on how refreshed you look. Of course, you let them know how good it was to get away and how wonderful you feel.

74. Kick Up One's Heels

What's Going On? Ask the class the following questions:

What do you think the man is doing? Why do you think he's doing this? What is he doing with his feet? What is he doing with his arms? How do you think he feels, judging from his facial expression? Do you have any idea why he is feeling this way? What do you think is enabling the man to stay up in the air?

The Ball's in Your Court   Ask the class the following questions:

Name some occasions that call for a celebration. In what ways can people celebrate? Have you ever gone out to celebrate a special occasion? If so, describe your celebration. What were your feelings at the celebration? What do you think a person does when he "kicks up his heels"? Name some factors (such as music) that might contribute to people's enjoyment of a celebration.

It's Up to You   Present this situation to the students for discussion:

What would you say about a person who finally got the promotion he had been waiting for and then went out to celebrate the occasion?

Play It by Ear   Have the students compose (orally or in writing) a skit or dialogue based on the following situation:

Stan has been playing tennis ever since his early teens. He had a natural ability for the sport, and through hard work he became good enough to enter professional competitions. After two unsuccessful attempts to win the national cup, he was finally able to beat out all the other contenders for the coveted prize. Needless to say, he was overcome with joy and invited his friends to go out for a night on the town.

75. Bury the Hatchet

What's Going On?   Ask the class the following questions:

What are the two men armed with? What are they tossing into the hole? Why would they throw away their weapons? What do you think they intend to do? Do you think that the two men have the same feelings about resolving their dispute? Judging from their facial expressions, would you say that the men are angry with each other? In which direction are the men walking? What does this fact indicate about their attitudes toward each other?

The Ball's in Your Court   Ask the class the following questions:

What is a hatchet ordinarily used for? Can a hatchet hurt someone? Could it be used as a weapon? What is another name for a hatchet? Name some other tools that serve functions similar to those of an ax. What do dogs often like to do with bones? When something is buried, is it gone and forgotten? Explain your answer. When you have had a disagreement with someone, what steps do you usually take to resolve it? In your opinion, what would be a good way to settle a dispute?

It's Up to You   Present this situation to the students for discussion:

What would you say about two people who had been quarreling violently and finally decided to make up?

Play It by Ear   Have the students compose (orally or in writing) a skit or dialogue based on the following situation:

Joshua and Yoshi are the best of friends. They have known each other since childhood and have shared common interests. Recently, they had a major falling-out over a woman whom they both liked. Each man would become angry whenever she paid more attention to the other man than she did to him. However, the source of the conflict was removed when Joshua and Yoshi learned that the woman had eloped with a third man. It didn't take long for Joshua and Yoshi to reestablish their friendship.

76. Paint the Town Red

What's Going On?   Ask the class the following questions:

How are the two people dressed? Describe their clothing. Why do you think they are dressed like that? What is the man carrying? What is the woman carrying? What does the man have in his mouth? What do you suppose they're going to do? Do you see any contradiction between the way the people are dressed and what they are carrying?

The Ball's in Your Court   Ask the class the following questions:

What does the color red suggest to you? Would you say that it is a sad color or a happy, bright color? What are some holidays that are associated with the color red? In your opinion, what would an evening "on the town" consist of? Do all people enjoy themselves in the same ways? What are some different ways in which people enjoy themselves? Do you see any relationship between *kicking up one's heels* and *painting the town red*? Under what circumstances could each expression be used?

It's Up to You   Present this situation to the students for discussion:

It's your first visit to Chicago. Your friends take you on a tour of the city and then they take you out dining and dancing at some of the better-known discos. After you return home, a colleague asks you what you did on your first night in Chicago. What would you answer?

Play It by Ear   Have the students write an essay or speech based on the following situation:

Mr. and Mrs. Jones are in your city on vacation. They have both been working very hard and have not had a vacation for years. Mr. Jones knows the city quite well and wishes to visit not only its many cultural centers but also some of the finer restaurants. He plans a whirlwind tour of the city. Describe some of the places Mr. and Mrs. Jones will visit and some of the things they will do.

77. Get Away Clean

What's Going On?   Ask the class the following questions:

Who's in the bathtub? What are the men doing there? What is one of the men using on his back? Judging from their appearance, would you say that these men need a bath? Why or why not? What are they wearing on their faces? What is on the floor next to the bathtub? What would you say the two men do for a living? Who is approaching the bathtub? What is he holding in his hand? What do you think he intends to do?

The Ball's in Your Court   Ask the class the following questions:

What are some different ways in which people keep clean? What do people do when they want to escape punishment? Can you think of a "getaway scene" from a movie that impressed you? If so, describe it. Think of some other situations in which a person might flee in order to avoid being caught. Have you ever tried to "get away with something"? If so, were you successful in escaping punishment? Describe the situation. Do you think that all people must eventually pay for their wrongdoings, even if they are not immediately caught? Explain your answer. What is the relationship between the expressions *face the music* and *get away clean*?

It's Up to You Present this situation to the students for discussion:

Last year there was a major bank robbery in our town. The authorities were unable to find a single trace of the robber. What could be said about the robber?

Play It by Ear Have the students compose (orally or in writing) a skit or dialogue based on the following situation:

Yesterday a burglary took place at the Golden Gate Fields Racetrack. While the last race was going on, a group of well-dressed men approached the cashier's cage. They gained entrance to the cage by claiming that they had been sent from company headquarters to check over the books. Once inside the cage, they were able to overcome the security guards and make off with a great amount of money. They had planned their getaway with such care that the authorities have not been able to capture them. Nevertheless, the burglary is a major topic of conversation at the police station.

78. Come Alive

What's Going On? Ask the class the following questions:

In what is the man lying? Why do you suppose he was put there? Does he look like a normal person? What's different about him? What is he doing now? Judging from his facial expression, how would you say he is feeling? Why do you think he feels this way? What do you think his previous condition might have been?

The Ball's in Your Court Ask the class the following questions:

What are some activities that can brighten up an occasion? In your opinion, what factors can make a party dull and boring? Have you ever attended a celebration or a festive occasion when you really did not feel like going? If so, what happened? Were you able to brighten up, or did you spend the evening sulking? Did any one particular thing cause a change in your mood? If you are feeling gloomy or out of sorts, what usually helps you to feel better?

It's Up to You Present this situation to the students for discussion:

Pretend that it's your birthday. You think that nobody has remembered, so you feel quite dejected. Suddenly, your friends walk in with many presents and a big cake. How do you react?

Play It by Ear Have the students compose (orally or in writing) a skit or dialogue based on the following situation:

You have just passed back an examination to the students in your English class. Generally speaking, the grades were not very high and the students are feeling rather sad. You realize how the students are feeling and make some reassuring comments to the class. They begin to feel much better, especially when you tell them you will give another test on the same material and record only the higher of the two grades. After this announcement, the students relax and begin to joke and make light-hearted remarks with each other.

All's Well That Ends Well

I. Select the best idiom to complete each sentence. In some cases, more than one answer is possible.

1. Now that they've paid off the mortgage on their house, they can_____
   _____.
   a. bury the hatchet
   b. kick up their heels
   c. make a big splash

2. What a relief! Final exams are finally over! Let's go out and_____
   _____.
   a. get away clean
   b. kick up our heels
   c. paint the town red

3. Come on, stop moping about your recent misfortune. _____
   _____! It's not like you to let a problem like that get you down.
   a. Come alive
   b. Let's bury the hatchet
   c. Let's go make a big splash

4. You say you_____?
   Sure. I paid cash for it and avoided the interest charges.
   a. feel like a million dollars
   b. are sitting pretty
   c. got it for a song

5. Well, how did you enjoy your vacation to Bermuda?
   Great! I_____! Now I'm ready to get back
   to work.
   a. am sitting pretty
   b. have the world by the tail
   c. feel like a million dollars

6. The teacher exchange program between the United States and the Soviet Union was quite
   successful. The group of American teachers_____.
   They were even invited by the Ministry of Education to speak on American education.
   a. made a big splash
   b. got away clean
   c. buried the hatchet

7. There's no doubt about it. After winning the lottery they_____
   _____!
   a. were sitting pretty
   b. came alive
   c. felt like a million dollars

8. The band of thieves who got into the building_____.
   It's too bad the security guards weren't more alert.
   a. got it for a song
   b. kicked up their heels
   c. got away clean

9. Look, why don't we_____and start all over again?
   All this quarreling isn't going to get the problem solved.
   a. come alive
   b. bury the hatchet
   c. go paint the town red

10. I don't understand it. He's acting as if he_____,
    and I know for a fact that he just lost his job.
    a. made a big splash
    b. had the world by the tail
    c. were sitting pretty

Name_____ Date_____

II. Complete the sentences with idioms from the list below. Make any necessary changes in grammar and wording.

for a song   make a splash
have the world by the tail   sitting pretty
feel like a million dollars kick up one's heels
bury the hatchet   paint the town red
get away clean   come alive

1. Thank heavens he didn't_____this time.
   _____(escape punishment)

   He's been wanted for a series of crimes up and down the coast.

2. We were able to pick up a beautiful lace tablecloth at the rummage sale

   _____. It would have cost us three times
   _____(for very little money)

   as much in any department store.

3. No wonder he feels that he's_____. He just
   _____(successful and happy)

   received a promotion at work and an extra bonus for being the top salesman!

4. Everyone was bored during the speeches, but they all_____
   _____(cheered up)

   when it was time to announce the winners of the door prizes.

5. Joseph was considered a prodigy on the violin and had_____
   _____(been successful and attracted attention)

   _____in the music world when he was young. As he grew older, however,

   he gave up his music and developed other interests.

6. Several opposing factions within the same political party decided to

   _____and work together to defeat
   _____(put an end to bitter feelings)

   the candidate from the rival party.

7. If we had inherited as much money as they did, we would

_____, too. It would be great to be
                (be in a fortunate position)

financially independent.

8. After hearing about her engagement to Tom, all of June's friends at the office decided to take

her out to_____. They had
             (go out and have a good time)

dinner at an expensive restaurant and then went to see the latest musical comedy. It was a

wonderful evening out.

9. When Professor Saunders heard that his manuscript was going to be published by a major firm,

he_____. It was refreshing
         (felt wonderful)

to see him smiling and in such good spirits.

10. Very frankly, she has every reason to_____.
                (celebrate an occasion)

The doctors informed her that her test results were negative, so she will not need that major

operation she was fearing.

III. Complete the crossword puzzle using the clues below.

Across
1. bury the_____
4. _____the world by the tail
6. _____pretty
7. make a_____
10. get away_____

Down
2. come_____
3. kick up one's_____
5. feel like a_____dollars
8. for a_____
9. paint the town_____

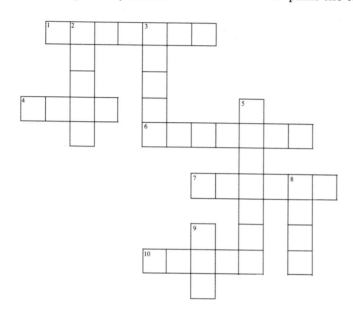

Answer Key

I.
1. b
2. b or c
3. a
4. c
5. c
6. a
7. a or c
8. c
9. b
10. b or c

II.
1. get away clean
2. for a song
3. got the world by the tail (or sitting pretty)
4. came alive
5. made a splash
6. bury the hatchet
7. be sitting pretty
8. paint the town red
9. felt like a million dollars
10. kick up her heels (or paint the town red)

III.

Section Eight

Do Your Best

79. Toot One's Own Horn

What's Going On? Ask the class the following questions:

What is the man in the illustration doing? When people hear fanfare on a horn, how do they usually react? What does fanfare generally signify? Judging from the man's clothing, what would you say his title is? According to the banner on the horn, how does the king feel about himself? Do you think that a person of his position should have any cause to boast about himself? Why or why not?

The Ball's in Your Court Ask the class the following questions:

In what ways do people usually boast about themselves? What reasons might they have for doing so? Do you think it is better for a person to talk about his own accomplishments or to have someone else talk about them? Based on your personal experience, have you found that people who praise or show off their own accomplishments are justified in doing so? Are you talented in any particular field? Do people know that you have this talent? If so, how have they found out? What do you think about a person who boasts about his accomplishments without having reason to do so?

It's Up to You Present this situation to the students for discussion:

What would you say about a person who constantly talks about himself and boasts about his accomplishments?

Toot Your Own Horn Have the students compose (orally or in writing) a skit or dialogue based on the following situation:

You have just come home from an evening out with several of your friends. Your roommate asks if you enjoyed yourself. You explain that the evening went well but that you were somewhat bothered by one of the members of the group, who has a reputation for being a Casanova. When he started to brag about how women could not resist his charm and good looks, you just couldn't keep on listening to him and decided to come home early.

80. Stick to One's Guns

What's Going On? Ask the class the following questions:

Where is the man? How is he maintaining his position on the barrel of the cannon? Does he intend to stay in this position? Why do you think so? How is the man dressed? Describe his clothing. Do you see a relationship between the man's uniform and the cannon?

The Ball's in Your Court Ask the class the following questions:

Have you ever had to maintain a position that was unpopular or unacceptable to a majority of people? If so, did you give in to the popular, majority opinion, or did you try to defend your point of view? Why would a person refuse to change his mind or to give in to the opinion of others? Under what circumstances would you give in to pressure from someone else? Give an example of a situation in which someone has maintained his or her position on a controversial matter.

It's Up to You Present this situation to the students for discussion:

What would you say about a person who did not agree with the majority opinion concerning a controversial matter and who refused to change his opinion in spite of pressure from the group?

Toot Your Own Horn Have the students compose (orally or in writing) a skit or dialogue based on the following situation:

You are having a conversation with your friend Bill. He tells you that he was extremely upset with his final grade in history. He complains that the teacher failed to give him credit for the extra work he did on the Civil War and that the teacher made errors in recording two of Bill's exam grades. The teacher refused to change the grade even after Bill confronted him with evidence of his error. Bill refused to give up and went to the principal with his complaint, because he felt justified in requesting that the grade be changed. After reviewing the evidence, the principal ruled in Bill's favor. Bill never doubted for a single minute that he was right, so he refused to accept a grade he did not deserve.

81. Get the Ball Rolling

What's Going On? Ask the class the following questions:

What season is shown in the picture? Describe the weather during this season. What do you think the man with the little snowball wants to do? Why is he rolling the snowball? Why is the other man resting? What did he accomplish? How did he accomplish his goal? Why is one snowball so big and the other so small?

The Ball's in Your Court Ask the class the following questions:

If a person has a long-range goal, what is it necessary to do in order to reach that goal? Can you explain the saying "a good beginning is a good end"? Have you ever had to do something that was difficult for you? How did you feel about starting on the project? Was it hard to get started? Describe the situation. How do you feel when you accomplish something difficult? Have you ever put off doing something? If so, what was the reason?

It's Up to You Present this situation to the students for discussion:

John has been putting off cutting the lawn. It's beginning to look very untidy. His wife reproaches him for letting it grow so tall. How might she tell him to start taking care of the matter?

Toot Your Own Horn Have the students create a skit based on the following situation:

Imagine that you are a member of the football team and you have practice on Saturday mornings. One Saturday you arrive for practice a half hour early. Many other members of the team are in uniform and are sitting around making general conversation. You sit with them and discuss the events of the week. All of a sudden you hear a whistle. The coach has arrived and wishes to begin practice right away. He urges the team to get out on the field.

82. Mind One's P's and Q's

What's Going On? Ask the class the following questions:

What are the letters P and Q doing in this picture? To whom are they pointing? What reason would they have for doing this? Do the letters seem subdued or emphatic? What is their attitude toward the boy? Does it appear that the boy has done something wrong? Could he have said something to displease the P and Q?

The Ball's in Your Court Ask the class the following questions:

When someone behaves improperly, what reaction can that person expect from a parent or supervisor? Do you think children should be told how to behave? If so, under what circumstances, and by whom? In your opinion, what would constitute improper or unacceptable behavior in a child? What about in an adult? Are there occasions when an adult's behavior can be improper or unbecoming? If so, give some examples. How would you define "improper behavior"? Give some examples of improper behavior. Has anyone ever reproached you for your table manners or for showing improper etiquette on a particular occasion? Give some examples of situations that illustrate what proper etiquette should be.

It's Up to You   Present this situation to the students for discussion:

How would you admonish a child who was being impolite and talking disrespectfully to another person, especially to an adult?

Play It by Ear   Have the students compose (orally or in writing) a skit or dialogue based on the following situation:

During a baseball game, the players often have reason to dispute an umpire's judgment. For example, one day Steven's team is in a game that is tied, four to four. Steven has just hit the ball far out into left field. It looks like a home run! He runs very fast around the bases, but just as he is coming into home plate the catcher tags him out. Steven thought he was safe, so he begins to argue the decision of the umpire. The umpire warns Steven to mind his manners and tells him he'll be thrown out of the game if he doesn't stop arguing.

83. Hang On

What's Going On?   Ask the class the following questions:

Where is the store? Would you say that the store is in a safe position? Why not? How do you think it got into this position? What are the two men doing? How do you think they got there? What do their facial expressions tell you? How long do you think they will be able to maintain their position? What would happen if they let go of the building?

The Ball's in Your Court   Ask the class the following questions:

Give an example of an adverse situation. What would a person have to do in order to live through an adverse situation? What character traits would you say are necessary for survival in such a situation? Have you ever been in a situation where you had to persevere until help arrived? Do you see a relationship between the idioms *bite the bullet* and *hang on*? What do these expressions have in common? Do they differ in any way? Explain your answers.

It's Up to You   Present this situation to the students for discussion:

A friend of yours is attending college but has gotten tired of studying and wants to drop out of school right before graduation. Knowing that it is in her best interest to finish school, what advice would you give her?

Play It by Ear   Have the students compose (orally or in writing) a skit or dialogue based on the following situation:

Your soccer team has had a great deal of success in past seasons, but this season your team has lost three games in a row. The losses have really discouraged the players, and everyone fears that the team might end up in last place. The coach, however, has great faith in the team. He knows the strength and talent of the players and refuses to be overcome by thoughts of defeat. He urges his players to be patient and to have faith, for he is certain that eventually they will overcome their losing streak.

84. Give It One's Best Shot

What's Going On?   Ask the class the following questions:

What does the man have in his hand? What does he intend to do with it? How do you think he feels? What do you think has happened to make him feel this way? What do you think he previously tried to do to the TV set? Does it appear that he was successful?

The Ball's in Your Court   Ask the class the following questions:

Do you think that trying very hard to accomplish something is necessarily a guarantee of success? Why or why not? Give some examples of situations in which great effort is required for success. "Great effort" can be either physical or mental. Give some examples of physical and mental effort. Have you ever tried your hardest to accomplish a certain goal? Were you successful, or did you fail to achieve your goal in spite of your best efforts? Think of some other people you know. Would you say that they had to go through a lot to get where they are? Would you call them successful? Explain your point of view.

It's Up to You   Present this situation to the students for discussion:

What could you say to someone who wants to become a cosmetologist but does not know if he will be successful in passing the course?

Play It by Ear   Have the students compose (orally or in writing) a dialogue or skit based on the following situation:

Phillip is one of the best salesmen at the company where he works. He is conscientious, as well as pleasant and outgoing. He has never had problems in meeting his bimonthly sales quota. As a matter of fact, on many occasions he has even exceeded his quota. Nevertheless, in spite of his best efforts, he has fallen short of his goal this month and he feels somewhat depressed. What do you think he will say when his boss calls him in to discuss his recent sales figures?

85. Make Ends Meet

What's Going On?   Ask the class the following questions:

What animals are shown in the illustration? What are they trying to do? Does it look like they are successful? Would you say that it was difficult for them to accomplish their goal? Why? In the illustration, *end* is a reference to what part of the animal's body?

The Ball's in Your Court   Ask the class the following questions:

Is it hard or easy to make things meet end to end? If possible, give some examples. What must people do in order to meet their financial obligations? Is it easy or difficult to meet such obligations? Who might have the most trouble in making ends meet? Explain your answer. What do many families do when one salary is not enough to cover ongoing financial obligations? Why do you think that more women have jobs now than at any other time in history? Who can afford not to work? Do you think these people are happy? Explain your answer.

It's Up to You   Present this situation to the students for discussion:

What would you say about a person who was generally short of money and had difficulty in meeting his financial obligations?

Play It by Ear   Have the students compose (orally or in writing) a dialogue or skit based on the following situation:

Ted Smith had a good, secure job with an automobile manufacturing company. His wife Elizabeth was employed at an import-export firm. Since the Smiths' combined income was rather high, they were able to purchase many luxuries. Recently, Ted was laid off because of cutbacks in personnel. Now that they must live off of one salary, the Smiths are experiencing great financial difficulties. One evening they discuss their situation and come to the conclusion that they will have to borrow money in order to meet their monthly payments.

86. Get the Jump on Someone

What's Going On?   Ask the class the following questions:

What kind of animal is jumping over the man? Why do you suppose it can jump so high? What is its natural habitat? Name some other animals from this region. How is the man dressed? What would you say he is preparing to do? Does he appear to be in competition with the kangaroo? If so, what is the sporting event? Does the kangaroo have an advantage over the man? If so, in what respect? Who do you think will win the race? Why do you think so?

The Ball's in Your Court   Ask the class the following questions:

What are some ways in which one person can have an advantage over another? What might a person do to gain an advantage over another person? What factors in a person's background might give him an advantage over someone who lacks either the natural ability or the training of the other? Have you or any of your friends ever been in a situation where someone was successful in "beating you out"? If so, describe the situation.

It's Up to You   Present this situation to the students for discussion:

Tran, a photographer, had inside information about the arrival of an important foreign dignitary. As a result, Tran and a reporter friend of his were the only members of the press to greet the dignitary upon his arrival. What would you say about their position in relation to the competition?

Play It by Ear   Have the students create a skit based on the following situation:

Comitac, a computer company, was just starting out in the production of microchips. The market is highly competitive but very lucrative. The engineers at Comitac developed a new memory chip for microcomputers that was certain to be in great demand. The president of the company met with her employees to remind them how important it was to maintain total secrecy about this chip until it could be marketed, so that Comitac could gain and maintain an advantage over the other computer firms.

87. Pull Strings

What's Going On?   Ask the class the following questions:

What is on the end of each string? To what are the strings attached? What is the man trying to do? What is the reaction of the man in the uniform? How can you tell? What type of uniform is the man wearing? Why do you think the man with the money is offering it to the other man? What might he want in return? Do you think that the man in the uniform will remain indifferent to the money for long?

The Ball's in Your Court   Ask the class the following questions:

Do you think that people are often influenced by money? In your opinion, is money most often used to influence people to do something positive or something negative? Explain your answer. Do you think that money corrupts people? Why or why not? In what other ways can people be influenced? Do you think that people in important positions ever use their influence to do favors for people? What kinds of favors might they do? Have you ever asked a favor of someone in an important position? If so, was this person able to help you achieve a goal that you would not have been able to achieve on your own? Have you ever tried to help another person by putting in a good word for him with someone who respects your opinion?

It's Up to You   Present this situation to the students for discussion:

If you knew an important official of a company, and a relative of yours wanted a job in that company, what could you do to try to help your relative get that job?

Toot Your Own Horn   Have the students compose (orally or in writing) a skit or dialogue based on the following situation:

You have been playing the violin ever since you were a child. You have studied with fine teachers and now you are ready to play professionally. You hear of a vacancy in the first violin section of the Metropolitan Symphony Orchestra. You know that many highly qualified musicians will be competing for the job. You, too, have high qualifications. However, you are also planning to call on your uncle to help you, since he is a personal friend of the president of the symphony association.

88. Spread Oneself Too Thin

What's Going On?   Ask the class the following questions:

What type of machinery is the little man sitting on? What is this type of machinery ordinarily used for? What has happened to the man on the ground? In his present condition, will he be able to function normally? Why not? Before he ended up in his present condition, what was the man doing?

The Ball's in Your Court   Ask the class the following questions:

What happens when a person tries to do too many things at once? Does the quality of some projects suffer when a person becomes involved in other projects? What is required to successfully complete a project? Have you ever become involved in so many activities that you could not complete them all? Do you think that some people can handle more than others? Why do you think so?

It's Up to You   Present this situation to the students for discussion:

What happens to a person when he becomes involved in too many activities and finds it difficult, if not impossible, to successfully complete them all?

Toot Your Own Horn   Have the students compose (orally or in writing) a skit or dialogue based on the following situation:

Your friend Joseph has been feeling very tired lately. When he comes home, all he wants to do is sleep. You realize that he is helping out his relatives overseas by sending them some money every month. In order to do this, he has had to take on two part-time jobs in addition to his full-time job. As a friend, you advise Joseph that he is becoming involved in too many outside activities and that eventually the quality of his work at his primary job will begin to suffer.

89. Go to Bat for Someone

What's Going On? Ask the class the following questions:

What are the two men holding? Why do you suppose they are holding it together? What do they intend to do with it? Do they appear to be at odds with each other, or would you say that they have something in common? How can you tell? In what game is a bat used? In the illustration, does it appear that one of the men needs help in order to hit the ball? Do you think that two men can do the job better? Explain your answer.

The Ball's in Your Court Ask the class the following questions:

What do you know about the game of baseball? Describe how the game is played. Name and describe some other games that are played with a ball. When a player is injured in some way during a game, is his position left vacant? What happens? Have you ever "stood in" for anyone? If so, under what circumstances? How were you able to help that person out? Have you ever needed someone to vouch for the validity of your actions? If so, describe the situation. What is the meaning of the expression "in unity there is strength"?

It's Up to You Present this situation to the students for discussion:

If someone accused one of your friends of doing something wrong and you knew that the accusation was false, what would you do for your friend?

Play It by Ear Have the students compose (orally or in writing) a skit or dialogue based on the following situation:

Andrew's little brother Tim had been playing in the backyard and had gotten his tennis shoes and jeans quite dirty when he accidentally fell onto a mound of dirt while chasing a ball. Tim's mother had told him to be careful not to get dirt on his clothes since they were going to be visiting friends that afternoon. When she saw Tim she became angry and began to scold him for not listening to her. However, Andrew, who had witnessed the whole incident, came to his brother's aid and asked his mother not to be so severe with Tim since it was an accident. He pointed out that Tim had really been very careful to stay away from the muddy areas of the yard and that he did not intentionally disobey her.

90. Duck Soup

What's Going On? Ask the class the following questions:

What animal is shown in the illustration? Where is he sitting? What is he doing? Why does he have a napkin around his neck? What is he eating? What eating utensil is he using? Judging from his expression, how do you think he feels? Does he appear to be having any trouble with his meal?

The Ball's in Your Court Ask the class the following questions:

What other animals live in the same habitat as a duck? Name some other eating utensils and tell how they are used. What kind of background helps to make a job easier? Do you think that previous training and experience help? Explain your answer. What types of jobs do you do well? Can you explain why? What types of jobs are difficult for you? Why? Do you know how to make duck soup? Is it easier or more difficult to make than other kinds of soups? Why?

It's Up to You   Present this situation to the students for discussion:

A man in a restaurant asked the pianist to play a popular tune for him. The pianist did so immediately and effortlessly. What would you say about the pianist's ability to fulfill the man's request?

Play It by Ear   Have the students compose (orally or in writing) a skit or dialogue based on the following situation:

A student in chemistry class is having a hard time completing all the required experiments. Another student, Jill, is just the opposite. She is very talented in chemistry and works through all the experiments in record time. For Jill, chemistry is no problem. She offers to help the student who is having so much difficulty in the class.

All's Well That Ends Well

I. Select the best word or phrase to complete each sentence. In some cases, more than one answer is possible.

1. Nowadays, it's difficult to make ends meet. With the rising costs of higher education and consumer goods in general, many couples have a lot of trouble_____

_____even if the husband and wife both work.
   a. sending their children to college
   b. paying all their bills
   c. doing something effortlessly

2. Come on, guys. Let's get the ball rolling. If we don't_____

_____, we'll be here all night!
   a. start getting this down on paper
   b. push it
   c. get going

3. "It may be hard for you to go down this slope on one ski, but for a pro like him, it's duck soup."
   "True, but any way you look at it,_____."
   a. it still is easy
   b. it takes a lot of concentration
   c. you shouldn't eat soup after skiing

4. It's not always easy to stick to your guns in the face of adversity, but you should_____

_____if you know you're right.
   a. not change your mind
   b. give in
   c. stand up for what you believe in

5. Surely you must realize that you spread yourself too thin when you agreed to_____

_____.
   a. become chairman of the committee
   b. be careful of what you were saying and doing
   c. lose weight

6. Rick says he gave it his best shot when he was in law school, but_____

_____.
   a. he tried very hard to succeed
   b. he always missed the target
   c. he still failed the bar exam

7. It's not hard to see why Peggy's going around tooting her own horn. If you had just won first place in the music competition, you would probably be_____

_____, too.
   a. bragging about it
   b. playing a musical instrument
   c. traveling a lot

8. When you're in another country it's a good idea to mind your P's and Q's. If you don't, people

   are likely to think that_____.
   a. you are illiterate
   b. you are rude
   c. you take great care in what you say and do

9. Adam was one of the best news reporters on the staff. He was always getting the jump on his

   colleagues. None of them could quite figure out how_____

   _____.
   a. he constantly beat them to a story
   b. he was able to jump higher than they could
   c. he could arrive on the scene before they did

10. Gil admits that he pulled some strings to get a personal audition with the symphony conductor.

   He was friends with Bruce, the conductor's assistant, and he asked Bruce_____

   _____.
   a. to use his influence with the conductor to get Gil the audition
   b. to accompany him to the audition
   c. to tie some string around his instrument

11. _____! If you just hang on, things are bound to get better.
   a. Be careful
   b. Be patient
   c. Try harder

12. I appreciate the fact that you went to bat for me._____

   _____, you helped me out of a very tight spot.
   a. Since I was too tired to play myself
   b. By exerting your influence
   c. With your athletic ability

II. Complete the sentences in the following dialogues with idioms from the list below. Make changes in grammar and wording as needed.

toot one's own horn	stick to one's guns
get the ball rolling	mind one's P's and Q's
hang on	give it one's best shot
make ends meet	get the jump on someone
pull strings	spread oneself too thin
go to bat for someone	duck soup

Dialogue 1

Carmen: Are you going to the dance this weekend?

Sonia: Well, I'm going to_____
(try my hardest)

if Ana doesn't_____.
(get the advantage over me)

Carmen: What do you mean?

Sonia: Well, I was sure that Carlos was going to ask me to go, but now that Ana has come into

the picture I'm not so sure. He seems to be somewhat attracted to her. I've been hinting

that I'd like to go, but he hasn't asked me yet.

Carmen: Listen, if I were you I'd go see Carlos and_____
(let him know just how good I am)

a little bit. And then I'd go to Ana and tell her to_____.
(watch out what she says and does)

After all, Carlos has always taken you everywhere. You just

_____. Don't let Ana ruin your weekend.
(strongly maintain your position)

Sonia: I'm glad I talked to you about it. I'm going to follow your advice.

Carmen: Well, what are you waiting for? Come on,_____!
(start doing something about it right away)

Dialogue 2

Hiroshi: Hey, Serge. You haven't been looking so good lately. What's up?

Serge: I guess I've been_____.
                                         (taking on more than I can handle)

I took another job last week, and I haven't been getting much sleep. I've had some

extra expenses and it's been hard to_____.
                                            (pay all my bills)

Hiroshi: Gee, I'm sorry to hear that. You know, maybe I can help.

Serge: How?

Hiroshi: Well, if you can_____for a week or so,
                                (persevere)

I can_____with my department head.
             (help you out by pleading your cause)

A new, high-paying job in your field will be opening up very soon. You'd be perfect for it!

Serge: Look, I wouldn't want you to go_____
                             (exerting influence with your boss)

for me if you have any doubts about my ability to handle the job.

Hiroshi: How can you say that?! Knowing you as I do, I'd say it would be

_____for you!
(very easy, nothing at all)

Serge: Wow! I feel better already. I can't thank you enough.

III. Fill in the blanks below, then find and circle the missing words in the puzzle. Be sure to look horizontally, vertically, and diagonally.

1. toot one's own_____ (boast)

2. get the ball_____ (initiate action)

3. _____on (persevere)

4. make_____meet (pay one's bills)

5. pull_____ (exert influence)

6. go to_____for someone (help out and support someone)

7. _____soup (easy, effortless)

8. spread oneself too_____ (become involved in too many activities)

9. get the_____on someone (get the advantage over someone)

10. give it one's best_____ (try hard)

11. _____one's P's and Q's (take care in speech and action)

12. stick to one's_____ (maintain one's position)

q	s	c	j	t	r	d	u	c	k	u	t	i	y
e	a	h	o	r	n	s	o	v	w	y	b	a	t
g	z	a	o	q	o	c	t	w	p	s	d	u	z
s	f	n	p	t	h	l	e	f	u	t	h	i	n
j	e	g	b	p	j	i	l	b	x	r	n	b	a
n	d	c	a	q	l	r	c	i	k	i	r	s	j
m	i	n	d	o	m	v	d	e	n	n	f	t	u
l	h	g	m	e	n	d	s	f	i	g	u	k	m
m	n	b	o	n	k	l	g	d	j	s	w	v	p
k	a	g	u	n	s	z	m	y	g	x	h	l	x

Answer Key

I. 1. a or b   5. a   9. a or c
    2. a or c   6. c   10. a
    3. b   7. a   11. b
    4. a or c   8. b   12. b

II. **Dialogue 1**

give it my best shot, get the jump on me, toot my own horn, mind her P's and Q's, stick to your guns, get the ball rolling

Dialogue 2

spreading myself too thin, make ends meet, hang on, go to bat for you, pulling strings, duck soup

III. 1. horn   5. strings   9. jump
     2. rolling   6. bat   10. shot
     3. hang   7. duck   11. mind
     4. ends   8. thin   12. guns

```
q  s  c  j  t  r  d  u  c  k  u  t  i  y
e  a  h  o  r  n  s  o  v  w  y  b  a  t
g  z  a  o  q  o  c  t  w  p  s  d  u  z
s  f  n  p  t  h  l  e  f  u  t  h  i  n
j  e  g  b  p  j  i  l  b  x  r  n  b  a
n  d  c  a  q  l  r  c  i  k  i  r  s  j
m  i  n  d  o  m  v  d  e  n  n  f  t  u
l  h  g  m  e  n  d  s  f  i  g  u  k  m
m  n  b  o  n  k  l  g  d  j  s  w  v  p
k  a  g  u  n  s  z  m  y  g  x  h  l  x
```

Section Nine

You Don't Say

91. Money Talks

What's Going On?   Ask the class the following questions:

What is in the bag? How is money depicted in the illustration? What do you suppose the "bag" is trying to do? How is the man reacting to the situation? Would you say that he's being tempted? How can you tell? Do you think that the man is showing weakness by allowing himself to be influenced by the money?

The Ball's in Your Court   Ask the class the following questions:

In what way(s) do you think that money can "talk"? Have you ever witnessed a situation in which money had the power to influence the outcome? If so, describe it. Do you believe that having money can give a person the upper hand in a situation? Why? Is this power positive or negative? Explain your answer. Do you think that most people are unduly influenced by money? What side of their personality does money bring out? In your opinion, what kind(s) of people would be most likely to be influenced by money?

It's Up to You   Present this situation to the students for discussion:

The man at the box office tells you that the best tickets for the game have already been sold; however, he unexpectedly "finds" two good tickets on the fifty-yard line after you slip him a ten-dollar bill on the side. What would you say about the "power" of that ten-dollar bill?

Play It by Ear   Have the students create a skit based on the following situation:

A couple has been waiting in line for a window table at a well-known restaurant. The hostess informs them that it will be another half hour before their table is ready. The man decides to take matters into his own hands since he does not wish to wait any longer. He approaches the maitre d' and slips him a twenty-dollar bill. The couple is seated immediately at one of the best tables in the restaurant.

92. Let Sleeping Dogs Lie

What's Going On?   Ask the class the following questions:

What animal is shown in the illustration? Describe the animal. What is he trying to do? Would you say that he is content? Who is bothering him? What is the man doing? How is the dog reacting to the man? What do you think the dog will do if the man insists on disturbing him?

The Ball's in Your Court   Ask the class the following questions:

What are some other animals or insects that you would not want to disturb? When is it better to leave things as they are? Why? How do you react when someone disturbs you and you wish to be left alone? Do you think it is better to keep quiet and not become involved in certain situations? In what circumstances would it be best to say something? When would keeping silent be the best course of action?

It's Up to You   Present this situation to the students for discussion:

What would you do if you discovered that your friend's wife was seeing another man? Would you tell him about it, or would you say nothing?

Play It by Ear   Have the students compose (orally or in writing) a skit or dialogue based on the following situation:

Everyone knows that Jane is hard to get along with. She is very sensitive, and people have to be careful of what they say to her for fear of "ruffling her feathers" (upsetting her). The other day Jane was wearing a very unbecoming skirt, but not even her best friend dared say anything to her. She knew how Jane would react to criticism and decided to keep quiet.

93. Shape Up or Ship Out

What's Going On?   Ask the class the following questions:

Where is the man standing? How can you tell? Describe the man's appearance. Would you say that he is physically fit? Describe his clothing. What is he doing with his hand? How does he seem to feel about his trip? Why do you suppose he is alone? Does he appear to be going willingly? Do you think he is going on vacation? What reasons do you have for your opinions?

The Ball's in Your Court   Ask the class the following questions:

When a child misbehaves, how do his parents handle the situation? What general courses of action can parents take to correct their children's behavior? How are adults treated when they do not behave properly? When someone behaves badly around you, what do you wish they would do? Why? If a person has a weight problem, what can he do to get back into shape? Do you see any relationship between *minding one's P's and Q's* and *shaping up or shipping out*? What idea do they have in common? How do they differ?

It's Up to You   Present this situation to the students for discussion:

A group of boys were misbehaving and making a commotion in a movie theater. The manager asked them to quiet down, but they continued to make noise. What could the manager say to let the boys know they would have to leave if they did not change their behavior?

Play It by Ear   Have the students compose (orally or in writing) a skit or dialogue based on the following situation:

Peter's parents have not been able to understand his behavior lately. He has been neglecting his studies and staying out late. His parents worry because he does not take the time to call and let them know where he is. He refuses to help out with the household chores, and when he is at home, he spends a great deal of time talking on the telephone or sitting in his room listening to loud music. Peter is old enough to show a greater sense of responsibility. His parents are fed up with his behavior and will tolerate it no longer.

94. If the Shoe Fits, Wear It

What's Going On?   Ask the class the following questions:

Who or what is shown in the illustration? Describe his overall appearance. What is the man looking at? Why? Would you say that he is comfortable with his acquisition? Judging from the appearance of the man, would you say that he is accustomed to wearing shoes? Why or why not?

The Ball's in Your Court   Ask the class the following questions:

If a shoe does not fit right, how would you feel about wearing it? What do you look for in a shoe? Do you always tell the truth? Do you ever admit that you have not told the truth or have blown something out of proportion? Do you think that a person should always tell the truth? Are there any circumstances in which it might be best not to reveal the truth? Explain your answer. If someone told you something that you knew was untrue, how would you react? If you were caught in a lie, would you admit it? In your opinion, are most people hesitant to accept responsibility for their actions? Why?

It's Up to You   Present this situation to the students for discussion:

George was involved in an automobile accident. He was clearly in the wrong, yet he refuses to admit that the accident was his fault. How could you ask him to admit the truth and take responsibility for what he did?

Toot Your Own Horn   Have the students compose (orally or in writing) a skit or dialogue based on the following situation:

You were quite fortunate to find a room in a big, old house when you came to study English in the United States. Besides yourself, there are three other students living in the house. Everyone is supposed to share equally in the routine maintenance of the house. One of your roommates, however, refuses to do his share of cleaning and washing the dishes. When you reproach Gene for ignoring his responsibilities, he becomes angry and denies the accusation. Everyone knows that your reprimand was justified and all demand that Gene admit that he was wrong and promise to fulfill his responsibilities in the future.

95. Different Strokes for Different Folks

What's Going On?   Ask the class the following questions:

Where are the people in the illustration sitting? How many people are there? What is each person holding? What are they doing? Are they all doing it the same way? Do they all seem to be enjoying what they are doing? How can you tell?

The Ball's in Your Court   Ask the class the following questions:

Do all people enjoy the same things? What are some things that you think most people enjoy and other things that you think most people dislike? What things do you enjoy doing most? What things do you particularly dislike? Do you believe that people have to enjoy doing the same things in order to get along with each other? Explain your answer. Have you ever disagreed with someone who felt that his was the only way to do something? If so, what happened? Is there usually only one right way to do something?

It's Up to You   Present this situation to the students for discussion:

You do not like swimming in the ocean, but you do enjoy swimming in a pool. What would you say to someone who wanted you to go swimming in the ocean with her?

Play It by Ear   Have the students compose (orally or in writing) a skit or dialogue based on the following situation:

Some relatives have come to visit your parents and have stayed overnight. In the morning your mother becomes rather frustrated when she tries to prepare breakfast for everybody. One wants cereal, another wants scrambled eggs, another wants French toast, and still another wants pancakes or waffles. Although your mother realizes that everyone has different tastes, it is difficult for her to accommodate everyone's desires. In desperation, she proposes that everyone go to a restaurant.

96. Bark Worse Than One's Bite

What's Going On?   Ask the class the following questions:

What animal is shown in the illustration? Is it large or small? Under normal circumstances, would you expect its bark to be loud or soft? What is the dog barking into? What is the function of the microphone? What is it attached to? When sound travels through a microphone and a speaker, what happens to the sound?

The Ball's in Your Court   Ask the class the following questions:

When someone addresses a large audience, what does he need in order to be heard? What happens to a sound when it is amplified? Is it exaggerated in any way? Do you ever say things that you don't really mean? Under what circumstances? When might a person threaten someone? Do people always intend to follow through with their threats? Have you ever been reprimanded by someone who was not really as fierce as he seemed when he was angry?

It's Up to You   Present this situation to the students for discussion:

Mrs. Thompson, a kind, gentle woman, got upset with a couple of boys and began yelling at them for playing tag on her front lawn. What would you say about her?

Toot Your Own Horn   Have the students compose (orally or in writing) a skit or dialogue based on the following situation:

Your father is very good about lending you the family car. You, in turn, have always been a careful, defensive driver. The other day you were driving along when a policeman pulled you over and began lecturing you rather severely for not having any taillights or properly working turn signals. You felt certain that he was going to give you a ticket, but in the end he let you go with a verbal reprimand. Fortunately, he was not really as mean as he sounded. That evening, you tell your father what happened.

97. Eyes Are Bigger Than One's Stomach

What's Going On?   Ask the class the following questions:

What animal is shown in the picture? How does the snake look to you? What do you think he has just done? Based on his size and shape, what would you say about the amount of food he ate? Why do you suppose he ate so much? Do you think he will suffer in any way because of the amount of food he ate?

The Ball's in Your Court   Ask the class the following questions:

In some countries burping is an acceptable sign of enjoying a meal. Is this true in the United States? Is it true in your native country? In America, when people overeat, how do they seek relief? Have you ever been to a buffet where everything was so well prepared and appetizing that you wanted to have some of everything? What did you do? What do you tend to do when you are really hungry? What effect would the sight of many appetizing dishes have on a person's desire to eat them, especially when one is particularly hungry?

It's Up to You   Present this situation to the students for discussion:

What would you say about a bunch of hungry men who ate too much and became ill?

Toot Your Own Horn

Have the students compose (orally or in writing) a skit or dialogue based on the following situation:

You have been working very hard around the house, doing some painting and cutting the grass. Your mother knows that you will be famished around dinner time, so she has prepared several of your favorite dishes. When you get to the dinner table, your mother places a normal portion of everything on your plate. You, however, are so hungry that you heap more food onto your plate, even though your mother has told you to eat what's on your plate before taking more. Unfortunately, you find that you cannot eat all the food on your plate. Your mother reprimands you for wasting food by taking more than you could really eat.

98. Put One's Money Where One's Mouth Is

What's Going On?

Ask the class the following questions:

Describe the man in the illustration. Does he seem uncomfortable, or do you think he is happy about what is going on? Do people ordinarily put money in their mouths? Do you see any connection between the location of the money and the value of the man's statements? Explain your answer.

The Ball's in Your Court

Ask the class the following questions:

Money has value. What other things have value? Would you say that money is the most important thing in most people's lives? What might be more important than money? Explain your answer. Where is money usually kept? When a person assumes a financial obligation, do you think he has a moral obligation to follow through with payment? Do you think people are obligated to follow through with their verbal commitments as well? What would you think of a person who does not stand by his word? Has anyone ever boasted to you that he could accomplish something difficult, then proved unable to follow through? What is the meaning of the saying "He's as good as his word"?

It's Up to You

Present this situation to the students for discussion:

Someone tells you that he is capable of learning a foreign language in six months. How could you tell him to prove the validity of his statement?

Play It by Ear

Have the students compose (orally or in writing) a skit or dialogue based on the following situation:

Lately Charles has been bragging about how good he is in gymnastics. He claims that he's really much better than anyone else in the class. He's even gone so far as to say that he can lift more weight than Jonathan, the biggest and strongest boy on the weight-lifting team. His friends find this hard to believe and challenge him to prove that he can do what he says he can.

99. The Early Bird Catches the Worm

What's Going On?

Ask the class the following questions:

Who is in the bed? Where is the bed? Who is approaching the bed? What does he have in his mouth? How would you say he feels about his accomplishment? While one of the birds has been busy, what has the other bird been doing? When the bird that's in bed finally gets up, do you think he will be as successful as his friend in finding food? Why or why not?

The Ball's in Your Court   Ask the class the following questions:

What is the best time to arrive when there is a sale at a department store? Why? In your opinion, is it always advantageous to arrive someplace early? Describe some situations in which being early would be advantageous and other situations in which it probably would not matter. Have you ever missed out on something because someone else got to it before you did? If so, describe the situation.

It's Up to You   Present this situation to the students for discussion:

There are a limited number of tickets available for the soccer championship game. What advice would you give to a friend who wants to get a ticket for the game?

Toot Your Own Horn   Have the students compose (orally or in writing) a skit or dialogue based on the following situation:

You are talking with some friends about a visiting dance ensemble from the Soviet Union. The dancers are known and admired for their technique and the originality of their dances. Needless to say, the dance troupe is very popular with audiences all over the world. You consider yourself fortunate to have obtained a pair of tickets for this evening's performance; however, you know that because of very heavy traffic you will have to leave for the performance at least an hour and a half before it starts. Otherwise, you won't find a parking place and you will have to pay a high fee to park your car in a public garage. Your friends agree that your plan is a good one.

100. People Who Live in Glass Houses Shouldn't Throw Stones

What's Going On?   Ask the class the following questions:

What is the house made of? Who is standing next to the house? What is he holding? What has he done to the house? Does it appear that the man will throw more stones? On what do you base your opinion? Judging from the expression on his face, would you say that the man is angry? What reason might he have for wanting to throw stones at the house? Do you think the owners of the glass house will retaliate in any way?

The Ball's in Your Court   Ask the class the following questions:

What does it mean to be in a vulnerable position? Do you think that a person who is in a vulnerable position should act in an aggressive manner? Explain your answer. In your opinion, what might prompt someone to say or do something rash? Have you ever been criticized for something you have said or done? Who criticized you? Was this person justified in his criticism? Was he himself without any faults? Could you have criticized that person for the same faults he claimed to have seen in you? Do you think that a person should not criticize other people if he himself has the same faults he is criticizing them for having? Explain your answer.

It's Up to You   Present this situation to the students for discussion:

Your brother constantly arrives late for dinner. One night you happen to arrive five minutes late and he criticizes you for doing so. What could you say to him about his actions?

Play It by Ear Have the students compose (orally or in writing) a dialogue or skit based on the following situation:

Soon after Evelyn began working in the office it became apparent that she was overly interested in the personal affairs of her coworkers. It was not long before she acquired a reputation for being a gossip. Of course, people began talking about her. Someone spread the word around that she had been going about with some quite unorthodox characters and behaving in a strange and erratic manner. When Evelyn found out that the whole office was talking about her, she became very angry and demanded that such gossip cease. Needless to say, more than one person reminded her of the things she had been saying about them.

101. All's Well That Ends Well

What's Going On? Ask the class the following questions:

Why do you suppose the man is running? What animal is chasing him? Describe the animal. What makes it so unique? How did the man get away? Was it difficult for him to do so? How would you say the man is feeling now? How would you describe his facial expression? Would you say that the man is safe now? Why? Why can't the animal follow him? Why would the animal be chasing the man in the first place? Judging from the look in the animal's eyes, do you think it is angry at not being able to continue the chase?

The Ball's in Your Court Ask the class the following questions:

In your opinion, which is worth more—something that comes easily or something that you have to try hard to achieve? Why? Have you ever been in a difficult situation? Was it easy or hard to get out of it? Was the outcome a happy one or a sad one? Describe what happened. Do you see any relationship between *out of the woods* and *all's well that ends well*? What do these idioms have in common? How do they differ? What is it necessary to do in order to become a doctor, lawyer, or engineer? Are the benefits that go with these careers worth the effort? Explain your answer.

It's Up to You Present this situation to the students for discussion:

Joanne is excellent at her job. Vincent does the same job, but receives a higher salary. Joanne tells her supervisor that she will quit unless she receives equal pay. Realizing Joanne's worth and the validity of her position, her supervisor grants her the raise in salary. What would you say about the fact that Joanne was successful in getting her raise?

Play It by Ear Have the students compose (orally or in writing) a skit or dialogue based on the following situation:

Ben went camping with his young son, Daniel. He told Daniel to stay close to the tent. However, Daniel felt adventurous and decided to go for a hike. When Ben called his son for dinner and the boy did not appear, he realized that Daniel had gotten lost. He immediately set out to look for the boy, and after five hours of searching in the wilderness he finally found his son. The boy was crying. He was feeling scared and guilty. He blurted out, "I should have listened to you!" Ben was greatly relieved to have found his son and was thankful that nothing had happened to him. He consoled Daniel by telling him not to worry and to be thankful that he was safe and well.

All's Well That Ends Well

I. Complete the sentences with idioms from the list below. Make changes in grammar and wording where needed.

money talks
shape up or ship out
different strokes for different folks
eyes are bigger than one's stomach
the early bird catches the worm
all's well that ends well

let sleeping dogs lie
if the shoe fits, wear it
bark worse than one's bite
put one's money where one's mouth is
people who live in glass houses
    shouldn't throw stones

1. I'll admit that I couldn't finish all the food I ordered at the restaurant last night. I guess_____
_____ .

2. Look, we've got enough trouble with our next-door neighbors as it is._____
_____ . If you antagonize them any more,
we're liable to have a war on our hands.

3. There's a big sale at that store tomorrow. If you get there early enough, you'll probably be able
to pick up everything you want at half price. Remember,_____
_____ .

4. _____ ! How much longer
do you think we're going to put up with this inattentiveness to detail?

5. Who are you to tell me I shouldn't lose my temper so often?_____
_____ ! Look how you overreact
when someone says or does something you don't like.

6. If you don't want to wait a long time for a good table in a restaurant, just remember that_____
_____ . Almost any maitre d'
will verify the truth of this statement.

7. Phillip said that he could quit smoking whenever he wanted to. We challenged him and told him
to_____ , since all
his previous efforts to stop had ended in failure.

8. They were accused of failing to carry out their duties. When they tried to deny it, we told them,
"_____ ." After all, why should
they try to hide the truth when everybody knows what's going on?

9. Don't pay attention to that old grouch._____
_____ . He yells a lot, but he wouldn't hurt a fly.

10. Well, just because it's raining doesn't mean I can't go swimming if I want to. No one asked you

to come with me. After all,_____

_____. You can stay home and read your book if that's what pleases you.

11. It was all worth it! We had a bit of a rough time going down the rapids, but_____

_____. We arrived safely on shore

and no one was hurt.

II. Match the situation in column A with the idiom in column B.

A

_____ 1. I don't understand why he's always criticizing me for the way I drive. He's got such a bad record that he had his driver's license suspended for a whole year.

_____ 2. Before the entire story could be published, it was necessary to get the remaining details from one of the informants. However, he kept silent until a group of reporters offered to pay him for the information.

_____ 3. My goodness! I felt so intimidated when Mr. Martinez was interviewing me. To tell you the truth, I almost walked out on him.

_____ 4. Jerry had been working on his car in the garage and didn't bother to clean up his mess when he finished. His father was terribly upset when he came home and saw the mess.

_____ 5. We were disappointed when we went on our picnic last Sunday because we couldn't find an unoccupied table on the picnic grounds.

_____ 6. The planning committee abandoned its plans to construct a freeway near a residential neighborhood because of the loud public outcry against the project.

_____ 7. Henry, there really is no harm in admitting that you are fluent in so many languages. Not everybody has your talent.

B

a. That's because you got there so late. Haven't you heard that the early bird catches the worm?

b. For the time being, it was decided to let sleeping dogs lie. There was no use antagonizing the voters.

c. After all, if the shoe fits, wear it. Be thankful that you have such a gift!

d. If that's so, let him put his money where his mouth is. Otherwise, he shouldn't expect anybody to believe him.

e. I guess you're right. Different strokes for different folks. But you don't know what you're missing.

f. Sure. We all know that money talks. It can open almost every door—if the price is right.

g. It's easy to see how he could have done that. His eyes might have been bigger than his stomach, but so were everyone else's.

_____ 8. Matthew says that he can get a date with a certain Hollywood movie star anytime he wants.

_____ 9. Just because we've never liked any topping on our dessert doesn't mean we're strange. You always have your dessert just the way you like it, and nobody says anything to you!

_____ 10. Pete had been looking forward to Thanksgiving dinner all day long. When it was finally served, it looked and smelled so good that he overloaded his plate and couldn't finish eating all the food he took.

_____ 11. I escaped with only the shirt on my back, but I'm thankful to still be alive.

h. You're absolutely right! He shouldn't be saying anything to you. People who live in glass houses shouldn't throw stones!

i. He told Jerry he'd better shape up or ship out, and said that there was no excuse for leaving all those dirty rags and tools for someone else to clean up.

j. He intimidates everybody at first, but as soon as you get to know him, you'll realize that his bark is worse than his bite.

k. All's well that ends well.

III. Complete the crossword puzzle using the clues below.

Across
2. money_____
4. let_____dogs lie
8. different_____for different folks
10. if the_____fits, wear it

Down
1. put one's money where one's_____is
3. shape up or _____out
5. the_____bird catches the worm
6. people who live in_____houses shouldn't throw stones
7. _____worse than one's bite
9. _____are bigger than one's stomach

Answer Key

I.   1. my eyes were bigger than my stomach
     2. Let sleeping dogs lie
     3. the early bird catches the worm
     4. Shape up or ship out
     5. People who live in glass houses shouldn't throw stones
     6. money talks

     7. put his money where his mouth is
     8. If the shoe fits, wear it
     9. His bark is worse than his bite
   10. different strokes for different folks
   11. all's well that ends well

II.   1. h   5. a   9. e
     2. f   6. b   10. g
     3. j   7. c   11. k
     4. i   8. d

III.

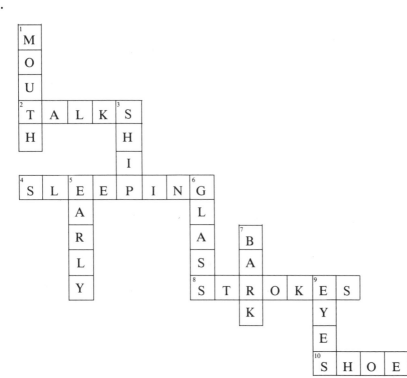

NTC ESL/EFL TEXTS AND MATERIAL
Junior High—Adult Education

Computer Software
Amigo
Basic Vocabulary Builder on Computer

Language and Culture Readers
Beginner's English Reader
Advanced Beginner's English Reader
Cultural Encounters in the U.S.A.
Passport to America Series
  California Discovery
  Adventures in the Southwest
  The Coast-to-Coast Mystery
  The New York Connection
Discover America Series
  California, Chicago, Florida, Hawaii,
  New England, New York, Texas,
  Washington, D.C.
Looking at America Series
  Looking at American Signs, Looking at
  American Food, Looking at American
  Recreation, Looking at American Holidays
Time: We the People
Communicative American English
English á la Cartoon

Text/Audiocassette Learning Packages
Speak Up! Sing Out!
Listen and Say It Right in English!

Transparencies
Everyday Situations in English

**Duplicating Masters and
Black-line Masters**
The Complete ESL/EFL Cooperative and
  Communicative Activity Book
Easy Vocabulary Games
Vocabulary Games
Advanced Vocabulary Games
Play and Practice!
Basic Vocabulary Builder
Practical Vocabulary Builder
Beginning Activities for English
  Language Learners
Intermediate Activities for English
  Language Learners
Advanced Activities for English
  Language Learners

Language-Skills Texts
Starting English with a Smile
English with a Smile
More English with a Smile
English Survival Series
  Building Vocabulary, Recognizing Details,
  Identifying Main Ideas, Writing Sentences
  and Paragraphs, Using the Context
English Across the Curriculum
Essentials of Reading and Writing English
Everyday English
Everyday Situations for Communicating in
  English
Learning to Listen in English
Listening to Communicate in English
Communication Skillbooks
Living in the U.S.A.
Basic English Vocabulary Builder Activity Book
Basic Everyday Spelling Workbook
Practical Everyday Spelling Workbook

Advanced Readings and Communicative
  Activities for Oral Proficiency
Practical English Writing Skills
Express Yourself in Written English
Campus English
English Communication Skills for Professionals
Speak English!
Read English!
Write English!
Orientation in American English
Building English Sentences
Grammar for Use
Grammar Step-by-Step
Listening by Doing
Reading by Doing
Speaking by Doing
Vocabulary by Doing
Writing by Doing
Look, Think and Write

Life- and Work-Skills Texts
English for Success
Building Real Life English Skills
Everyday Consumer English
Book of Forms
Essential Life Skills series
Finding a Job in the United States
English for Adult Living
Living in English
Prevocational English

TOEFL and University Preparation
NTC's Preparation Course for the TOEFL®
NTC's Practice Tests for the TOEFL®
How to Apply to American Colleges
  and Universities
The International Student's Guide
  to the American University

Dictionaries and References
ABC's of Languages and Linguistics
Everyday American English Dictionary
Building Dictionary Skills in
  English (workbook)
Beginner's Dictionary of American
  English Usage
Beginner's English Dictionary
  Workbook
NTC's American Idioms Dictionary
NTC's Dictionary of American Slang
  and Colloquial Expressions
NTC's Dictionary of Phrasal Verbs
NTC's Dictionary of Grammar Terminology
Essential American Idioms
Contemporary American Slang
Forbidden American English
101 American English Idioms
101 American English Proverbs
Practical Idioms
Essentials of English Grammar
The Complete ESL/EFL Resource Book
Safari Grammar
Safari Punctuation
303 Dumb Spelling Mistakes
TESOL Professional Anthologies
  Grammar and Composition
  Listening, Speaking, and Reading
  Culture

For further information or a current catalog, write:
National Textbook Company
a division of *NTC Publishing Group*
4255 West Touhy Avenue
Lincolnwood, Illinois 60646-1975 U.S.A.